SO-ARH-898

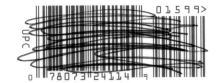

SCHOLASTIC

Interactive 3-D Maps: American History

Easy-to-Assemble 3-D Maps That Students Make and Manipulate to Learn Key Facts and Concepts—in a Kinesthetic Way!

Includes
Background
Information
& Activities

by Donald M. Silver and Patricia J. Wynne

■SCHOLASTIC

Interactive 3-D Maps: American History

Easy-to-Assemble 3-D Maps That Students Make and Manipulate to Learn Key Facts and Concepts—in a Kinesthetic Way!

by Donald M. Silver and Patricia J. Wynne

NEW YORK • TORONTO • LONDON • AUCKLAND • SYDNEY
MEXICO CITY • NEW DELHI • HONG KONG • BUENOS AIRES

Teaching
Resources

This book is dedicated to Michelle and Dominic Marra, whose lives were shortened because of cystic fibrosis, and to all children and adults who struggle every day for life and breath. May a cure soon be found.   —DMS

To all the explorers from the Land of Counterpane.   —PJW

Cover design by Adana Jimenez
Cover photo by James Levin/Studio Ten
Cover and interior artwork by Patricia J. Wynne
Interior design by Holly Grundon

ISBN: 0-439-24114-6
Copyright © 2005 by Donald M. Silver and Patricia J. Wynne

3 4 5 6 7 8 9 10   40   13 12 11 10 09

Contents

Introduction 4
Making the Maps and Pieces 5

The First People Arrive in America 6
Vikings Discover America 10
Columbus Lands in America 14
Cortés and Coronado Explore America 18
The French Explore North America 22
Cabot and Hudson Explore North America 26
Settlements at Roanoke and Jamestown 30
Voyage of the *Mayflower* 34
Slave Ships Cross the Atlantic 38
Piracy on the High Seas 42
Paul Revere's Ride 46
Washington Crosses the Delaware 50
Lewis and Clark Explore the West 54
A Ride Along the Erie Canal 58
The Trail of Tears 62
The Way West 66
Up and Down the Mississippi 70
The Underground Railroad 74
Messages Move From Coast to Coast 78
Civil War on the Sea 82
The Transcontinental Railroad 86
The Western Cattle Trails 90
Immigrants Flock to America 94
Building the Panama Canal 98
On the Road for Civil Rights 102
From Earth to the Moon 106

Resources for Teachers and Students 110

Introduction

You've probably had this experience—that when you touch and manipulate something, you understand it better than when you just hear or read about it. Research has shown that when students engage in a kinesthetic activity (e.g., touch and manipulate objects), the two hemispheres of their brains are stimulated simultaneously. This helps ensure that new information is stored in their long-term memory. Kinesthetic activities are especially helpful in making abstract concepts, such as American history, concrete. But how do you teach American history in a kinesthetic way?

Enter *Interactive 3-D Maps: American History*! The maps in this book highlight important events in our country's history, from the arrival of the first people in America to our leading role in the space race. Each map features one or more bold lines, which indicate routes that define a historical event. Students cut out, assemble, and insert illustrated pieces into the maps and move them along the routes, strengthening the connection in their minds between the maps and related people, geography, and historical events. Other illustrated pieces are captioned with informative text, enriching students' understanding of the historical event. (See page 5 for illustrated, easy-to-follow instructions on how to make the maps and related pieces.)

In each chapter of this book, you'll find the following sections:

Mapmaking: contains easy, step-by-step directions for assembling and placing additional illustrated pieces or other elements on the map

Map in Motion: describes where students insert the moving pieces and how to move them

Map Points: includes background information on the chapter's topic. Share some or all of this information with students.

Teaching With the Map: provides discussion questions to use with the map to teach the chapter's main concepts

More Mapwork: suggests other map-related activities to extend your students' investigation of the topic

Together, the interactive maps, detailed illustrations, background information, and lessons in this book are sure to make American history come alive for you and your students. In addition, students will gain skills in reading maps, understanding symbols, using a map scale, interpreting information, identifying directions, identifying topographical features, and locating places, states, regions, and continents. Finally, don't miss the extensive resource section at the back of the book to help you and your students explore American history further. Enjoy!

Making the Maps
and Pieces

1. Photocopy the two illustrated pages in each chapter.

2. Cut out the map sections along the thick black outlines. The section on the first page will always be the left or upper part of the completed map.

3. Tape the section on the second page to the first to complete each map, as shown.

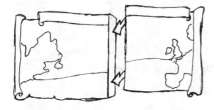

4. Cut out each moving piece and fold along the dashed midline between the two identical illustrations, as shown.

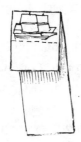

5. To make the base, fold up the side flaps along the dashed lines. Then fold the longer side under and tape in place, as shown.

6. Cut a slit along the bold arrow line(s) on each map. Insert the moving piece(s) between the slit so that only the illustrations show on the map surface. Make sure the piece(s) can move freely.

7. Cut out the additional pieces. Fold the pieces along the dashed lines so the text can be read easily, as shown. Tape the pieces on the map as directed on the "Mapmaking" instructions in each chapter.

8. You may want to mount each map on a piece of cardboard or construction paper to keep it sturdy. Make sure the moving pieces can still move freely along the slit.

The First People Arrive in America

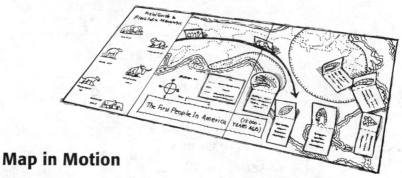

Map in Motion

This map shows what North America looked like thousands of years ago during the last Ice Age. Insert the hunters piece at the beginning of the arrow in Asia and the mammoth piece in front of the hunters. The hunters pursue the mammoth across the land bridge from Asia to North America. Continue moving the pieces until they reach the tip of the arrow.

Map Points

No one knows for sure when the first people reached North America. However, most scientists agree that it was at least 15,000 years ago during the last Ice Age. The climate in many parts of the world was so cold then that vast sheets of thick glacial ice formed and moved across parts of the continents, such as the northern part of North America. So much water was frozen in these glaciers that the sea level lowered. Land that is underwater today was uncovered. One stretch of exposed land appeared around the eastern tip of Siberia in Asia and west of Alaska. It included the Bering Strait, which now separates the two continents. Scientists have named this exposed land the Bering Land Bridge or Berengia.

The first people in North America were most likely Asian hunters, who crossed this land bridge in pursuit of animals they hunted for food and for fur. All of the animals pictured on the map migrated from Asia and have been extinct for thousands of years. Both animals and people moved down into present-day Canada through an ice-free corridor between two huge glaciers in North America. At the southern end of the glaciers, the climate was warm enough to melt the ice in summer. Both animals and people slowly fanned out across North America and down into present-day Mexico and Central and South America.

Scientists have found human and animal remains and tools in various parts of the Americas that date from 10,000 to 14,000 years ago. Among the tools

Mapmaking

1. Follow the instructions on page 5 for making the map, the moving pieces, and other pieces.

2. Display a current map of North America. Challenge students to place each piece near the location where it was found. Make sure these pieces don't block the movement of the mammoths or hunters as they move along the route.

3. Tape the pieces in place.

are spear points, scraping tools, and throwing sticks used by the ancient hunters. The first such spear point (about 13,000 years old) was discovered in 1932 in Clovis, New Mexico. Spear points have also been found in many sites across North America. Near such spear points, scientists often find fossilized bones of extinct animals, as well as the remains of snakes and other small animals the first Americans also may have hunted.

When the last Ice Age ended about 10,000 years ago, the glaciers melted, the sea level rose, and the ocean covered the land bridge between Asia and North America.

Not all scientists agree with the land-bridge theory. Some are searching for evidence that the first Americans arrived from Asia in canoes or kayaks. Others are studying the possibility that the first people paddled across the North Atlantic from what is today Portugal and Spain.

Teaching With the Map

1. **What does the map show?** *(It shows the first people crossing the land bridge from Asia to North America about 15,000 years ago.)*

2. **Why did people cross the land bridge?** *(They were hunting animals for food and furs. The animals crossed the land bridge ahead of the hunters.)*

3. **Why did a land bridge exist between Asia and North America 15,000 years ago?** *(During the last Ice Age, vast glaciers covered much of North America. Because so much water was frozen, the sea level fell, and the land between Asia and North America was exposed.)*

4. **What route did the people take in North America?** *(They moved down a corridor that had opened between two huge glaciers. This led them into what is today the United States.)*

5. **How do scientists know that the people fanned out across North America and south into Mexico and Central and South America?** *(Scientists have found tools, such as spear points, left behind by the hunters in different parts of the continent. They also have found remains of animals nearby that the hunters most likely killed.)*

6. **Do all scientists believe that the first people came to North America across a land bridge? Explain your answer.** *(No; some scientists believe the first people came to this continent by canoes or kayaks.)*

7. **Artifacts, such as the Clovis point and Folsom point, are often named after the locations where they were first discovered. Look at the fishtail-point piece. How do you think this type of spear point got its name?** *(Possible answer: The spear point resembles a fish, and its bottom is flared like a fishtail.)*

More Map Work

Challenge students to research and report on some aspect of the map. You may want to suggest the following topics:

- the last Ice Age
- the Pleistocene Era
- how glaciers form
- extinct North American animals
- the discovery of any of the tools and fossilized bones found in the Americas
- how scientists locate and date fossil remains of animals, people, and tools
- current theories about the first human migration to North America

Encourage students to be creative in their presentations. For instance, they might present their findings in the form of news reports, Web pages, magazine articles, Readers Theater plays, comic books, and so on.

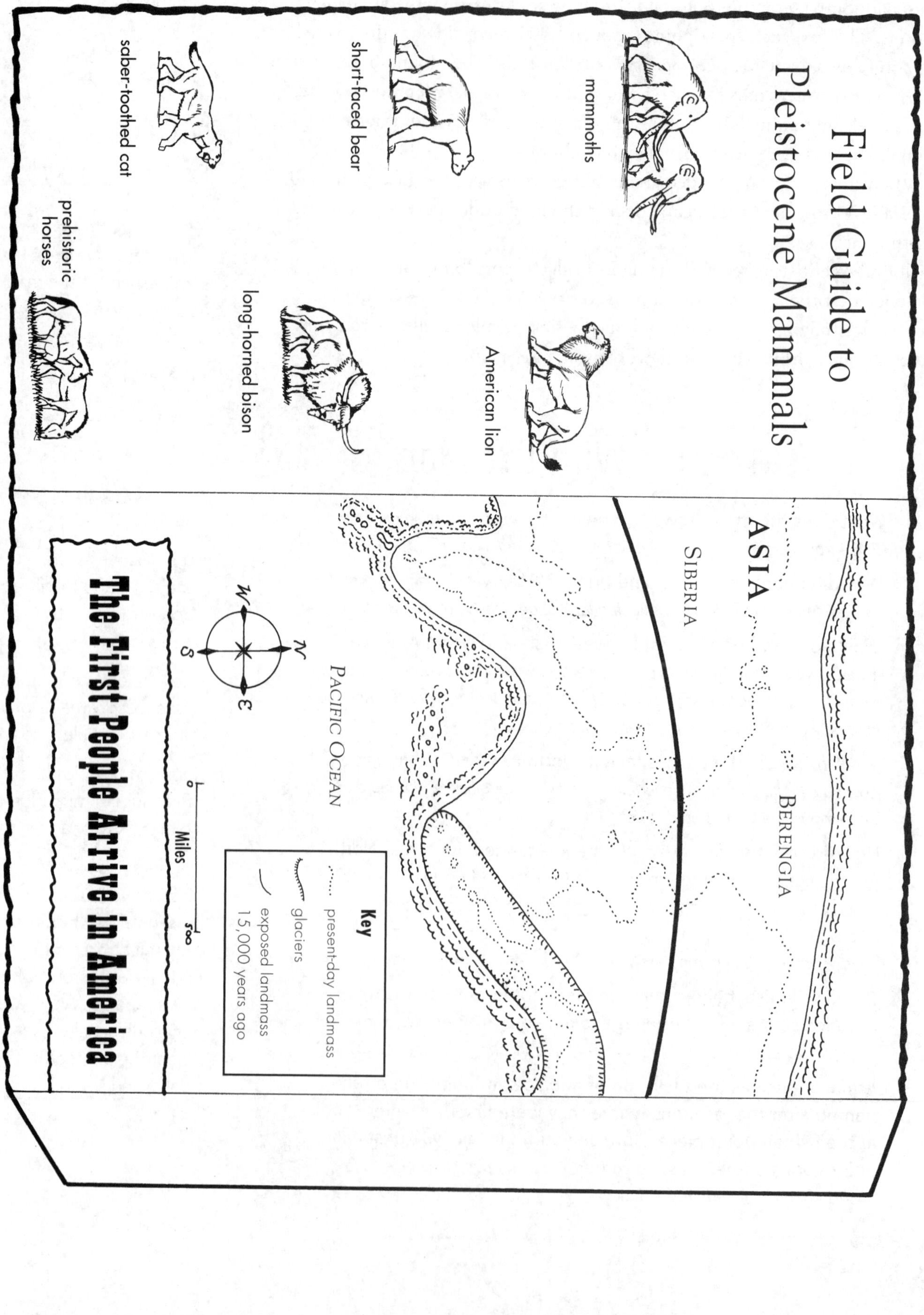
Field Guide to Pleistocene Mammals
mammoths
American lion
short-faced bear
long-horned bison
saber-toothed cat
prehistoric horses
ASIA
SIBERIA
BERENGIA
PACIFIC OCEAN
N
E
S
W
Key
present-day landmass
glaciers
exposed landmass 15,000 years ago
0
Miles
500
The First People Arrive in America

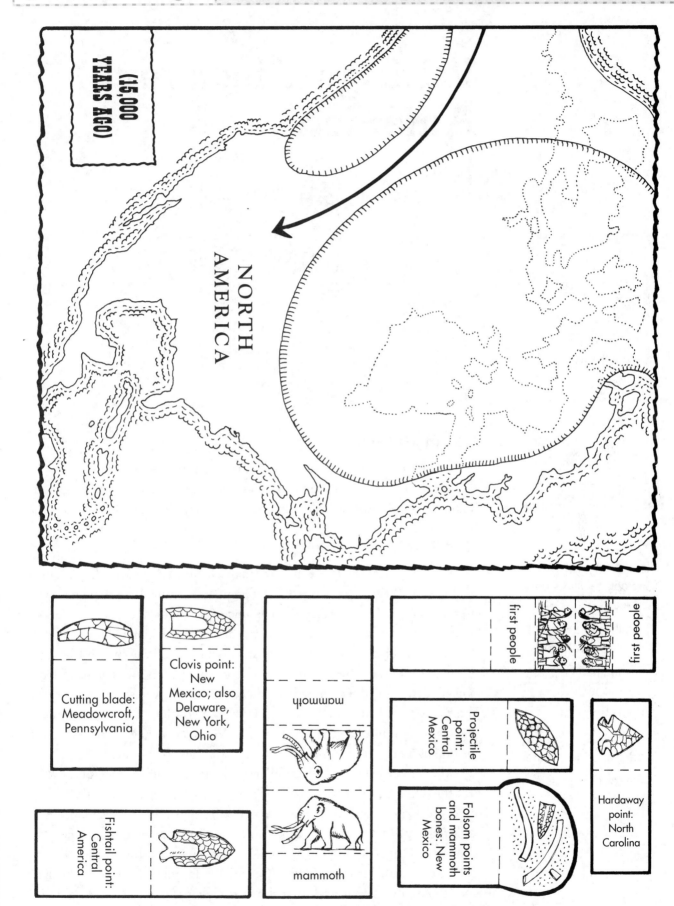

(15,000 YEARS AGO)

NORTH AMERICA

Cutting blade: Meadowcroft, Pennsylvania

Clovis point: New Mexico; also Delaware, New York, Ohio

mammoth

mammoth

Fishtail point: Central America

Projectile point: Central Mexico

Folsom points and mammoth bones: New Mexico

Hardaway point: North Carolina

first people

first people

Vikings Discover America

Mapmaking

1. Follow the instructions on page 5 for making the map, the moving pieces, and other pieces.

2. Cut out the two sod-hut pieces. Fold the ends of each piece and tape, as shown.

3. Tape the huts in their appropriate places on the map.

4. Tape the other pieces on the map as follows:

   • Erik the Red on Greenland

   • Leif Eriksson on his route

   • the grapes on Vinland

   • the solar compass as desired

Map in Motion

Insert Erik the Red's ship at Iceland and move it to the east coast of Greenland. Then insert Leif Eriksson's ship at the west coast of Greenland and move it to L'Anse aux Meadows in present-day Newfoundland.

Map Points

The Vikings were the first Europeans to reach North America. They originally came from what is now Norway, Sweden, and Denmark. Although they are often portrayed as brutal warriors and plunderers, Vikings were actually farmers, herders, hunters, craftsmen, shipbuilders, traders, and explorers. In the late 700s, they established settlements in parts of Europe and the British Isles.

Around this time, the Vikings also started building longships up to 75 feet long. To determine direction when sailing, they may have used a *solar compass*. The compass worked like a sundial and used the position of the sun and the angle of shadow to establish a bearing. The Vikings may have also relied on the position of stars or followed migrating whales to help them navigate.

In the middle of the 9th century, Vikings settled in Iceland. Around 980, Erik the Red sailed west from Iceland with a small group of men. They discovered a new land with green pastures that they named Greenland. After exploring parts of Greenland, Erik returned to Iceland and gathered families who wanted to settle in the new land. In that same year, Bjarni Herjolfsson and his crew sailed from Iceland to Greenland. En route, they were caught in a North Atlantic storm, and their ship was blown off course. They sighted forested land—most likely the coast of Newfoundland—before turning back and sailing east for Greenland.

Leif Eriksson, Erik the Red's son, heard stories about this forested land while growing up in Greenland. In the year 1000, Leif sailed west across the North Atlantic. He and his crew discovered Baffin Island before turning south to find the forested land (most likely present-day Labrador), which they called Markland. Finally, the Vikings sailed into a bay and landed at a green meadow known today as L'Anse aux Meadows. For about ten years, the Vikings explored Newfoundland and parts of Nova Scotia and New Brunswick. They called the entire region Vinland because wild grapes grew there.

Another explorer, Thorfinn Karlsefni, brought 160 men and women, including his wife, to Vinland. For a time, the Vikings traded with the indigenous people (the descendants of the first people to arrive in America), whom they called the Skraelings. Then the two groups began to fight. By 1010, the Vikings had abandoned North America and returned to Greenland.

The site of the green meadow, L'Anse aux Meadows in Newfoundland, was rediscovered in 1960. Soon thereafter, archaeologists uncovered ruins and remains of a settlement that dated back to the time of Leif Eriksson. Among the remains were evidence of sod huts built by the Vikings. Until this discovery, there had been no proof that the Vikings had indeed come to America 500 years before Columbus.

Teaching With the Map

1. **What does the map show?** (It shows the discovery of Greenland by Erik the Red and the discovery of North America by Leif Eriksson in the year 1000.)

2. **Who were the Vikings?** (The Vikings were Scandinavians who settled in parts of Europe before setting out to discover new lands to the west.)

3. **How did the Vikings navigate at sea?** (They used instruments such as a solar compass as well as the position of stars or the migratory routes of whales.)

4. **What did Leif Eriksson and his men discover as they sailed west across the North Atlantic?** (They discovered Baffin Island, Labrador, and Newfoundland.)

5. **What was L'Anse aux Meadows?** (It was the place where Leif and his men settled and built sod huts.)

6. **Why was the rediscovery of L'Anse aux Meadows in 1960 so important?** (It proved that the Vikings had arrived in America 500 years before Columbus did.)

More Map Work

Sagas, or stories, contained the first clues that the Vikings had settled briefly in America. The discoveries at L'Anse aux Meadows proved that the sagas weren't just fiction. Challenge students to report on one of the following Viking-related topics:

- artifacts found at L'Anse aux Meadows, including rune stones

- longships

- Norse sagas

- Viking women in America, including Freydis Eriksdottir

- length of Leif Eriksson's voyage and distances between Greenland and North America

Have students incorporate their maps in their presentations. For instance, they might make map pieces depicting artifacts and people.

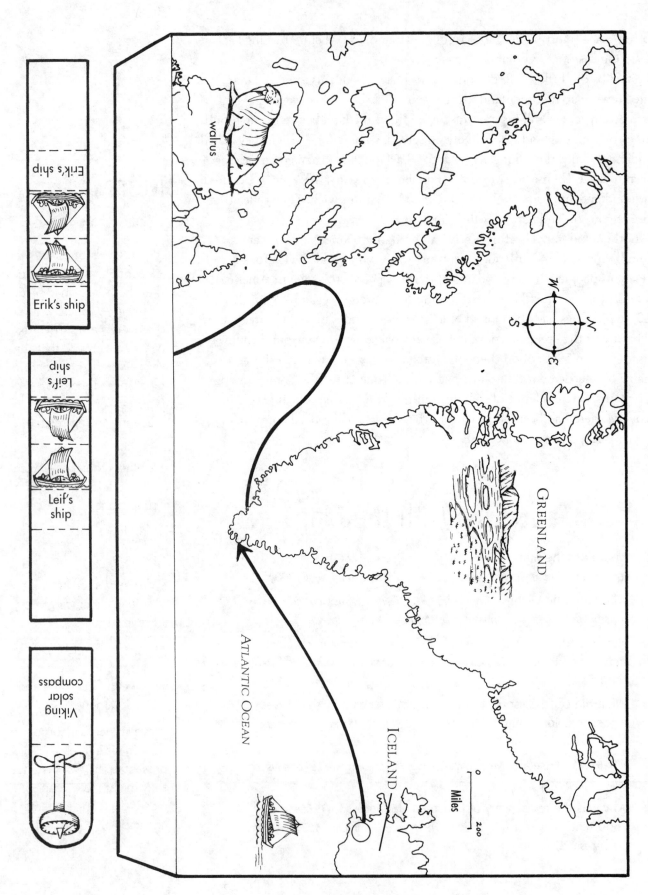

walrus

Erik's ship

Erik's ship

Leif's
ship

Leif's
ship

Viking
solar
compass

GREENLAND

ATLANTIC OCEAN

ICELAND

Miles

0

200

Interactive 3-D Maps: American History   Scholastic Teaching Resources

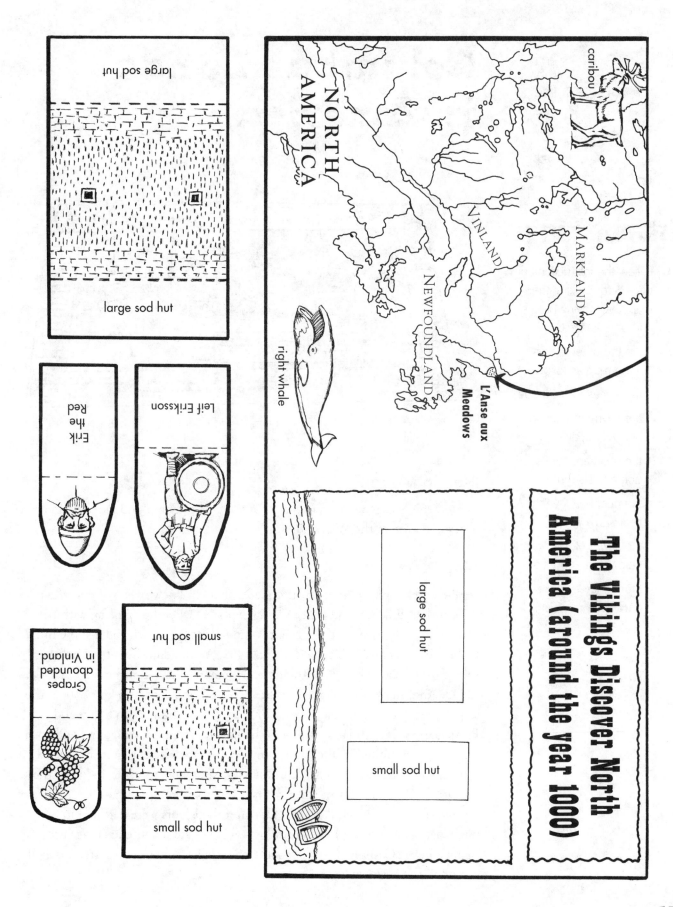

NORTH AMERICA

caribou

VINLAND

MARKLAND

NEWFOUNDLAND

L'Anse aux Meadows

right whale

large sod hut

large sod hut

Erik the Red

Leif Eriksson

Grapes abounded in Vinland.

small sod hut

small sod hut

large sod hut

small sod hut

The Vikings Discover North America (around the year 1000)

Columbus Lands in America

Mapmaking

1. Follow the instructions on page 5 for making the map, the moving pieces, and other pieces.

2. Tape the other pieces on the map as follows:

   - the spices over Europe

   - the payment treasure box over Spain

   - the quadrant above Columbus's route

   - the people above the final arrow tip

   - the *Santa Maria* sinking below that arrow tip

   - the manatee in the Caribbean

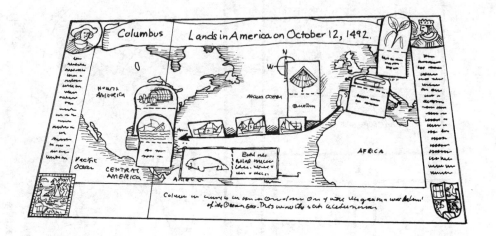

Map in Motion

Insert the *Niña*, the *Pinta*, and the *Santa Maria* at Spain and move them across the Atlantic to the West Indies.

Map Points

No one knows whether Christopher Columbus knew of the discoveries made by Leif Eriksson and other Viking explorers when he came up with the idea of sailing west from Europe across the Atlantic to reach India and China. Columbus was born in Genoa, Italy, in 1451. As an adult, he settled in Spain. Like most educated people of the time, Columbus knew that the world was round. And, since Marco Polo's visit to China, Europeans also knew about the spices, precious stones, gold, and silver found in the East. Both Spain and Portugal hoped to find a sea route to the East to avoid the dangerous and costly land route controlled by the Moors. In 1488, Portuguese explorers rounded Africa, but it took another 10 years for Vasco DaGama to reach India. In the meantime, Columbus spent seven years trying to drum up support for his idea of sailing west to reach the East. In 1492, after the Moors were defeated in Granada, Spain, Queen Isabella was persuaded by her counselors that both Spain and the Catholic Church could benefit if Columbus was correct. Isabella agreed to pay for his voyage.

Columbus secured three ships for his voyage. They were light, fast, easy-to-handle vessels. The *Santa Maria* might have been almost 90 feet long and held 40 men. The *Niña* and *Pinta*, with 24 and 26 men respectively, might each have measured close to 75 feet in length. On August 3, 1492, the three ships set sail from Palos, Spain. They stopped at the Canary Islands for provisions and then sailed west on September 6. The winds were favorable, and the sea was smooth. Columbus used a *compass* and a *quadrant* for navigation. With the quadrant, he could try to determine latitude by measuring the angle of celestial bodies, such as the stars, above the horizon.

At 2 A.M. on October 12, a lookout on the *Pinta* sighted land. A few hours later at dawn, Columbus stepped ashore on an unknown island. Greeted by the friendly inhabitants, he claimed the island for Spain and renamed it San Salvador. Columbus believed he had reached islands off the coast of Japan and called the natives *los indios*, which became translated as "Indians." In fact, Columbus and his crew had reached what are today the Bahaman Islands. For 96 days, Columbus explored the region, including the coasts of Cuba and Hispaniola, which he also claimed for Spain. He and his men were amazed by the variety of plants and animals there that they had never seen before.

On December 25, the *Santa Maria* hit a reef in the Caribbean and sank. A few weeks later, on January 16, 1493, the *Niña* and *Pinta* sailed home. Forty men remained behind to search for gold and other treasures for Queen Isabella and King Ferdinand.

More Map Work

The return trip to Spain was eventful. Challenge students to find out what happened to the *Niña* and the *Pinta* when they sailed home. Have them draw the ships' route on their maps, paying careful attention to where the ships separated. Then, ask students to research Columbus's three subsequent voyages to America and draw those routes on their maps. Remind them to use different markings (colors and lines) to distinguish the routes.

Teaching With the Map

1. **What does the map show?** *(It shows the voyage of Columbus's three ships across the Atlantic to America.)*

2. **What was Columbus's idea for getting to the East?** *(Columbus believed that by sailing west across the Atlantic he could reach the East and its riches.)*

3. **Why did Queen Isabella agree to pay for Columbus's voyage?** *(The queen's counselors persuaded her that if Columbus was correct, Spain and the Catholic Church would benefit greatly from the spices, jewels, and metals found in the East.)*

4. **What did Columbus find when he landed?** *(He found friendly people on the island, which he claimed for Spain, and new kinds of plants and animals.)*

5. **When did Columbus return to Spain?** *(After the* Santa Maria *was wrecked on a reef, Columbus and most of his men returned to Spain in January 1493.)*

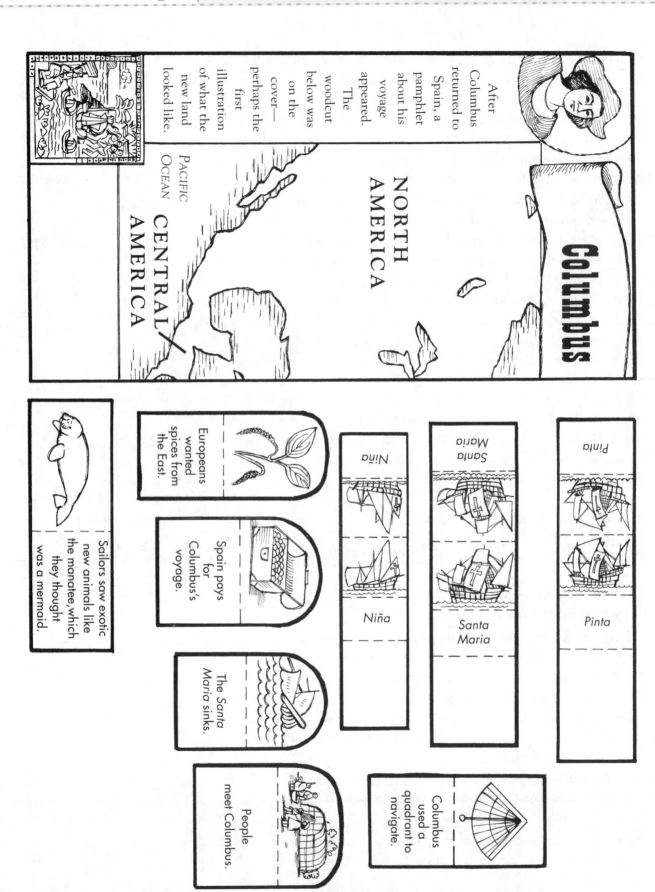

After Columbus returned to Spain, a pamphlet about his voyage appeared. The woodcut below was on the cover—perhaps the first illustration of what the new land looked like.

PACIFIC OCEAN

NORTH AMERICA

CENTRAL AMERICA

Columbus

Niña

Niña

Santa Maria

Santa Maria

Pinta

Pinta

Europeans wanted spices from the East.

Spain pays for Columbus's voyage.

The Santa Maria sinks.

People meet Columbus.

Columbus used a quadrant to navigate.

Sailors saw exotic new animals like the manatee, which they thought was a mermaid.

Lands in America on October 12, 1492

San Salvador in the Bahamas

SOUTH AMERICA

PACIFIC OCEAN

0
500
1000
1500
Miles

SPAIN

ITALY

EUROPE

AFRICA

King Ferdinand and Queen Isabella ruled Spain together. The Queen spoke to Columbus many times about the voyage he hoped to take. She helped convince Ferdinand that Spain should help Columbus.

Columbus was honored by the King and Queen of Spain. One of the titles they gave him was Admiral of the Ocean Sea. The crest at right was the symbol of Columbus's rank.

Cortés and Coronado Explore America

Mapmaking

1. Follow the instructions on page 5 for making the map, the moving pieces, and other pieces.

2. Tape the pueblo piece to the left of the mythical city on the map.

3. Cut out the great temple and fold along the dashed lines.

4. Fold the top flap over and tuck behind the top of the temple, as shown. Tape the side close, as shown.

5. Fold the bottom flap. Then tape the Great Temple in place below the map of Tenochtitlán.

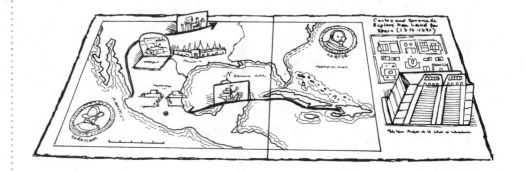

Maps in Motion

Insert Cortés's ship at Hispaniola and move it across the Gulf of Mexico to his landing in Mexico. Move Coronado and his soldiers from Mexico up into the Southwest United States.

Map Points

Following Columbus's successful voyages, Spain sent settlers to colonize the new lands it had claimed. Spain also embarked upon further exploration to claim as much land as it could in what seemed to be a "new world." Spanish explorer Hernando Cortés conquered much of what is today Mexico. When Cortés was 19, he sailed to the "new world" where he explored and fought for Spain on the islands of Hispaniola and Cuba. The governor of Cuba sent Cortés in search of gold and other riches that the Indians of Mexico might possess. In 1519, Cortés set sail in 11 ships. The ships carried several hundred men and some horses and dogs across the Gulf of Mexico and made landfall on Mexico's east coast. There, Cortés learned of an Aztec empire ruled by the emperor Montezuma.

This empire was made up of city states, with citizens who were primarily farmers growing corn, squash, and beans. The Great Temple in the center of the capital city of Tenochtitlán was sacred in the Aztec religion. Cortés and his men marched to the capital, which is now the site of Mexico City. Greeted as a god, Cortés soon arrested Montezuma, took control of the empire, stole gold and other riches from the Aztec people, and allowed his soldiers to destroy temples and other religious sites. When the Aztecs rebelled, Cortés called in reinforcements, destroyed the capital, and forced the Aztecs to an unconditional surrender under his full control.

A few years later, Francisco Vásquez de Coronado explored the American Southwest for Spain. He set out in search of the Seven Cities of Cibola that Indians and Spaniards, such as the explorer Alvar Nuñez Cabeza de Vaca, believed were rich in gold and jewels. Coronado had sailed with Antonio de Mendoza to Mexico, where the latter became viceroy, and Coronado was appointed a provincial governor. In 1540, Coronado led Spanish soldiers on horse and foot, along with Indian guides and servants, through parts of what today are Arizona, New Mexico, Texas, Oklahoma, and Kansas. Although they discovered Pueblo, Zuni, and other Native American villages, the Spaniards never found the mythical cities of Cibola. After suffering injuries when he fell off a horse, Coronado gave up the search and ordered his army to return to Mexico in 1542.

More Map Work

Extend students' understanding of Spanish exploration by having them research the following topics:

- the other parts of Mexico and Central America that Cortés visited

- the routes taken by the Coronado expedition, including the exploring parties

- the travels of Cabeza de Vaca

Instruct students to add their information to the Cortés and Coronado map.

Teaching With the Map

1. **What does the map show?** *(It shows the exploration of new lands by two Spanish explorers, Cortés and Coronado.)*

2. **Why did Spain send these explorers on their missions?** *(Spain wanted to claim more land and search for gold and other riches.)*

3. **What did Cortés explore?** *(He landed in Mexico and then marched to the capital of the Aztec empire.)*

4. **What does the inset to the right of the map show?** *(It shows the Aztec capital Tenochtitlán with the Great Temple in the center.)*

5. **What did Coronado search for?** *(Coronado and his men went in search of the mythical Seven Cities of Cibola.)*

6. **What did Coronado discover?** *(He and his men came across Pueblo, Zuni, and other Native American villages.)*

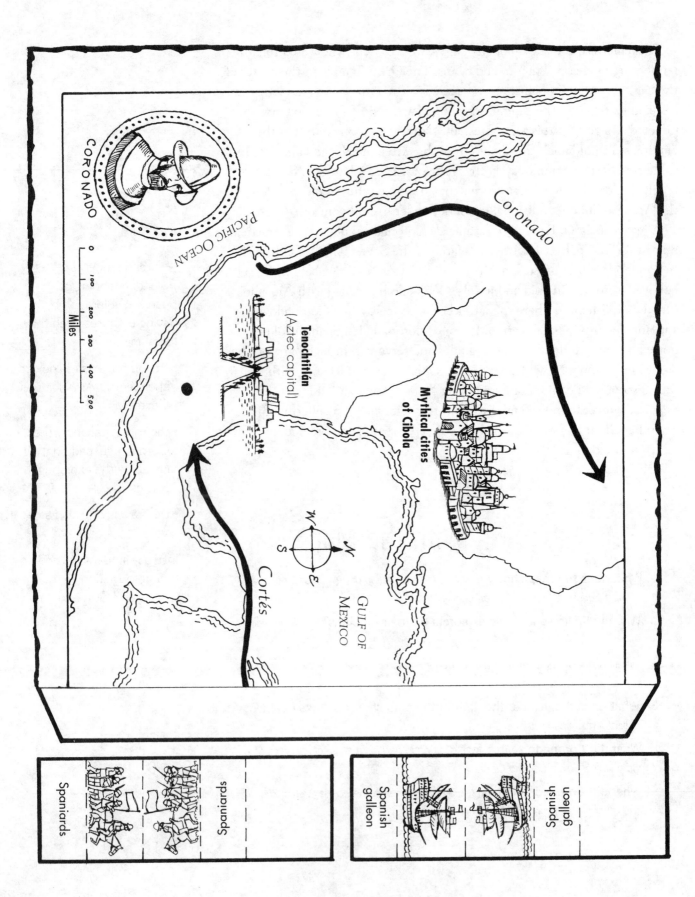

CORONADO

PACIFIC OCEAN

Coronado

0
100
200
300
400
500

Miles

Tenochtitlán
(Aztec capital)

Mythical cities
of Cibola

Cortés

GULF OF
MEXICO

N
W   E
S

Spaniards

Spaniards

Spanish
galleon

Spanish
galleon

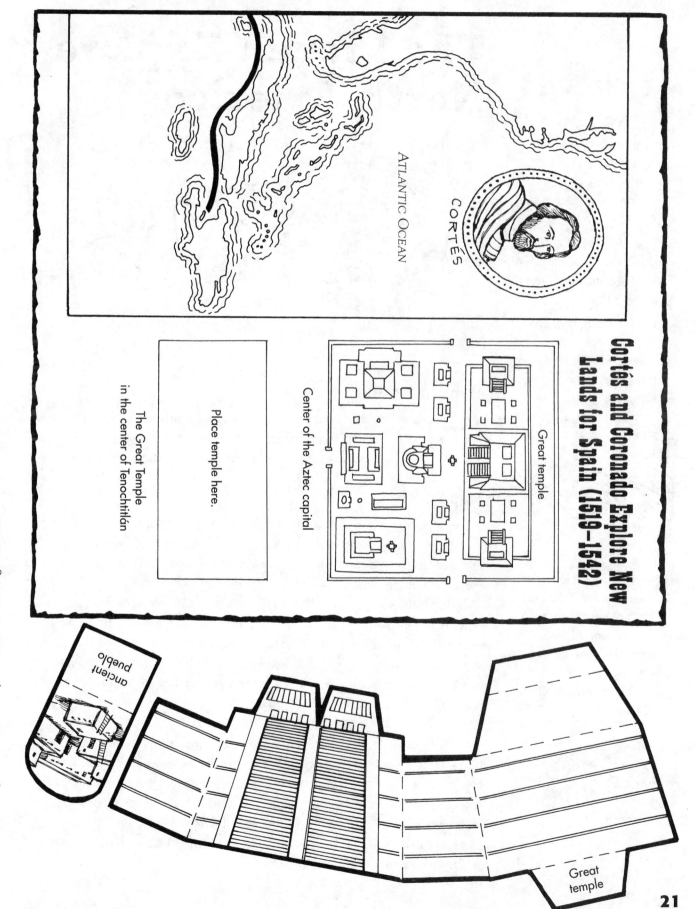

Cortés and Coronado Explore New Lands for Spain (1519–1542)

CORTÉS

ATLANTIC OCEAN

Great temple

Center of the Aztec capital

Place temple here.

The Great Temple in the center of Tenochtitlán

ancient pueblo

Great temple

Mapmaking

1. NOTE: There are two separate maps. Follow the instructions on page 5 for making the moving pieces and other pieces.

2. Tape the beaver piece above the St. Lawrence River and the longhouses below it.

3. Cut out the temple mound piece. Cut it open along the solid black lines. Then fold it along the dashed lines to form a pop-up, as shown.

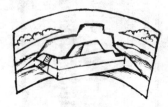

4. Curve the temple mound piece. Tape the ends of the canoe piece to each side of the temple mound to form a diorama, as shown. Tape it midway along the Mississippi River.

The French Explore North America

Maps in Motion

Move Cartier's ship from France, across the Atlantic Ocean, and down the St. Lawrence River in Canada. Move Marquette and Joliet's canoe from upper Michigan to the Mississippi River and farther south.

Map Points

Because France was in the midst of wars, it lagged behind Spain in exploring the Western Hemisphere. However, when word reached French king Francis I of Cortés's expedition in Mexico, he decided it was time to seek a French empire in America—and stop Spain from expanding further.

In 1534, the king sent navigator Jacques Cartier in search of land, gold, and other riches in North America. Francis I also wanted Cartier to find a western sea route to the Far East. Cartier sailed across the Atlantic with 61 men in two ships and eventually arrived at Gaspé Bay. There, he met Iroquois Indians led by Chief Donnacona and developed friendly trade relations with them. Cartier returned to France with two of Donnacona's sons—Domagaya and Taignoagny. They spoke of a great river and a kingdom beyond it.

Almost a year later, Cartier returned with the two Iroquois men, who guided him up the great river. The explorer named it for St. Lawrence. After setting up base camp, Cartier and a group of his men explored more in longboats. They reached an Iroquois village surrounded by cornfields. Near the village stood a mountain, which Cartier named Mont Royal. He had sailed up the St. Lawrence River to as far as where the city of Montreal stands today. Cartier and his men returned to the base camp.

More than a century later, in 1666, Jacques Marquette, a French missionary, was sent to America by the Jesuit Order of the Catholic Church. He worked in missions and among Native American tribes of the Great Lakes, including the Ottawa, Huron, and Illinois. When the French Governor General chose the explorer-trader Louis Joliet to determine whether the Mississippi River was a route to the Far East, Joliet invited Marquette to come along because of the missionary's knowledge of the Indians and their languages. In May 1673, Marquette and Joliet set out from St. Ignace in what is now northern Michigan. With five other men, they paddled in two canoes across Lake Michigan to the Fox River and up into Wisconsin. They moved overland to the Wisconsin River and then canoed to the Mississippi. Since the Mississippi flowed south, Marquette and Joliet concluded that it emptied into the Gulf of Mexico and not into the Pacific Ocean. The river wouldn't provide a water route to the Far East.

As the men paddled along the upper Mississippi, they encountered friendly Indians. These people were descendants of the Mississippian culture that had built great flat-topped earth mounds along the Mississippi River. Some of the mounds may have served as temples on which people stood and performed rituals. At the mouth of the Arkansas River, Joliet and Marquette learned that there might be Spaniards farther south. They turned back to avoid an attack. On their return trip, the men explored parts of Illinois.

Teaching With the Maps

1. **What do the two maps show?** *(One shows the exploration of the St. Lawrence River as far as Montreal by Cartier, and the other shows the exploration of the upper Mississippi River by Marquette and Joliet.)*

2. **Why did the French king send explorers to America?** *(Francis I wanted a western empire, gold and other riches, a water route to the Far East, and he wished to halt further Spanish expansion.)*

3. **What is Mont Royal?** *(A mountain named by Cartier, near a large Iroquois village)*

4. **Why did Joliet ask Marquette to join his expedition?** *(Marquette had worked among the Indians in the region and was familiar with their languages.)*

5. **Who built the great mounds along the Mississippi River?** *(The Mississippian culture, ancestors of the Native Americans Joliet and Marquette met, had built the flat-topped earthen mounds, some of which may have served as temples.)*

6. **Why did Marquette and Joliet turn back?** *(They wanted to avoid an attack by Spaniards.)*

More Map Work

Invite students to research one of the following topics:

- Cartier's third voyage of exploration in North America

- Marquette and Joliet's return trip up the Mississippi River

- the culture of the peoples that Cartier, Marquette, and Joliet met on their travels

- the Mississippian culture and the temple mounds

- other French explorers, such as Champlain and La Salle

In addition to producing reports, direct students to incorporate their findings on their maps.

Iroquois longhouses
lined the
St. Lawrence River.

Cartier saw
many beavers
along the river.
Soon, demand
for their fur rose
in Europe.

Cartier's
ship

Cartier's
ship

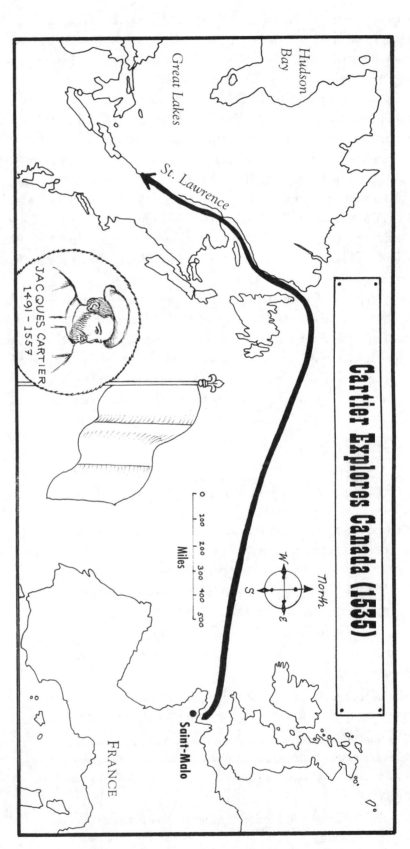

Hudson
Bay

Great Lakes

St. Lawrence

JACQUES CARTIER
1491 – 1557

Cartier Explores Canada (1535)

Miles

0
100
200
300
400
500

North
W
S
E

FRANCE

Saint-Malo

Interactive 3-D Maps: American History Scholastic Teaching Resources

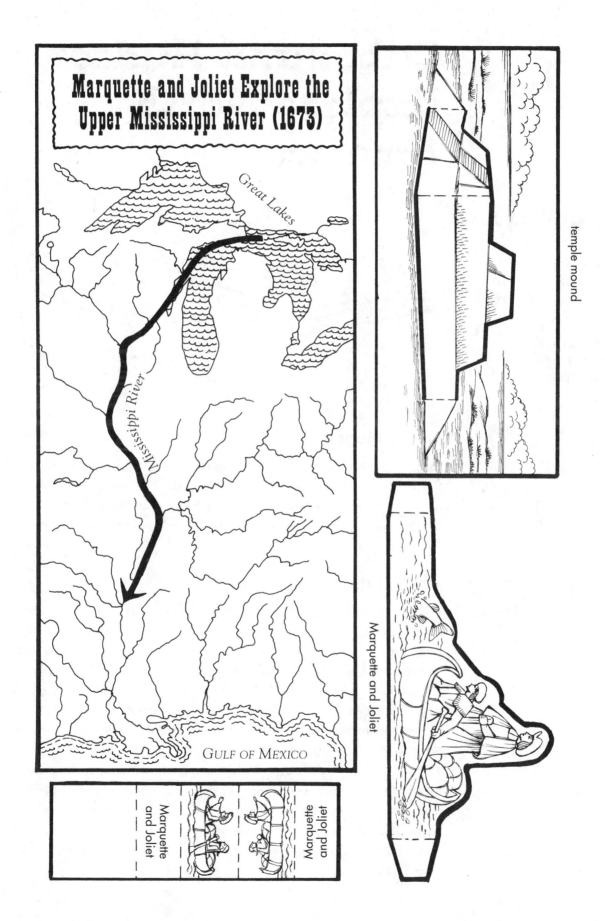

Marquette and Joliet Explore the Upper Mississippi River (1673)

Great Lakes

Mississippi River

GULF OF MEXICO

temple mound

Marquette and Joliet

Marquette and Joliet

Marquette and Joliet

Cabot and Hudson Explore North America

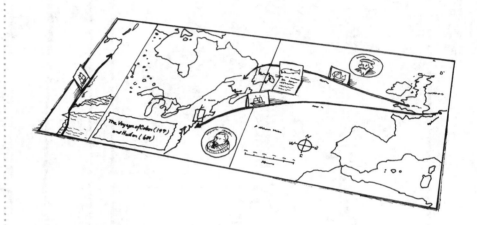

Mapmaking

1. Follow the instructions on page 5 for making the map, the moving pieces, and other pieces.

2. Tape the fish piece off the coast of Newfoundland.

Map in Motion

Move John Cabot's ship from England to the coast of Newfoundland. Then move Henry Hudson's ship (one *Half Moon* piece) from Holland, across the Atlantic, and down the northeast coast of the United States to Chesapeake Bay. Insert the other *Half Moon* piece on the map at the left and move it up the Hudson River.

Map Points

Both England and Holland sent explorers to America. In addition to claiming land and resources, rulers and merchants hoped to find a northwest passage, a shorter water route from Europe to the Far East. Although John Cabot sailed for England, he was born Giovanni Caboto in Italy. He became a sailor, trader, and mapmaker and lived in Spain with his family before moving to Bristol, England. There, Cabot sailed for merchants. Then, in 1496, he received permission from King Henry VII of England to sail north across the Atlantic in search of a northwest passage.

In May 1497, Cabot set sail with 20 men on the *Matthew*. They sailed west and reached the coast of present-day Newfoundland and Cape Breton Island, Nova Scotia. Cabot was certain he had reached the Far East, and he claimed the land for England. Returning to England, he brought news of the rich fishing grounds off the coast of Newfoundland, today known as the Grand Banks.

English explorer Henry Hudson also tried to discover a northwest passage that would connect Europe and Asia. Between 1607 and 1611, Hudson and his crews made four voyages west from Europe. Hudson was hired for the first voyage by an English trading company, and he sailed to an island about 700 miles from the North Pole. He was turned back by chunks of floating ice. Hudson's second voyage also met with failure because of ice floes.

Then, in 1609, he was offered a job by the Dutch East India Company. Hudson set sail with 20 men aboard the *Half Moon*, but because of stormy seas and bitter cold—and a crew dangerously close to mutiny—he steered south down the East Coast of the United States. Some of the crew went ashore in Maine to cut a pine tree trunk to replace the ship's weather-beaten mast. The *Half Moon* sailed down to the Chesapeake and Delaware Bays before Hudson changed course again for the north, where the *Half Moon* sailed into the harbor of a large river. Hudson was sure he had found the long-sought route to the Far East. However, by the time the ship reached the site of present-day Albany, New York, the river had become too shallow to proceed. Hudson was forced to turn back. He called the river the River of Mountains; today, it is known as the Hudson River. Based on Hudson's exploration, the Dutch claimed the land surrounding the river and soon built forts and trading posts on it.

Teaching With the Map

1. **What does the map show?** *(It shows exploration of the Canadian coast by John Cabot for England and the voyage of Henry Hudson for a Dutch company. Hudson explored the northeast coast of the United States down to Chesapeake Bay. Then he turned north and explored the Hudson River.)*

2. **What were Cabot and Hudson searching for?** *(They both were looking for land to claim and a northwest passage that would link Europe with the riches of the Far East.)*

3. **What information did Cabot take back to England?** *(Cabot brought back word of the land he had claimed as well as information about the rich Grand Banks fishing grounds off Newfoundland.)*

4. **Why did the *Half Moon* turn south instead of north in 1609?** *(The ship ran into bitter cold and stormy seas. Hudson's crew was also close to mutiny.)*

5. **What ended Hudson's exploration of the Hudson River?** *(The river became too shallow for the ship to proceed.)*

6. **What was the result of Hudson's third voyage to North America?** *(The Dutch were able to claim land on either side of the Hudson River and build forts and trading posts there.)*

More Map Work

Mystery surrounds the final voyages of John Cabot and Henry Hudson. Both explorers set out again for North America, but it seems likely that they perished. Challenge students to research the last voyages of Cabot and Hudson. Have them add the routes of these journeys to their maps. As an extension, suggest that students consult a present-day map of the Hudson River to locate and label New York City, Albany, West Point, and other places of interest on their maps.

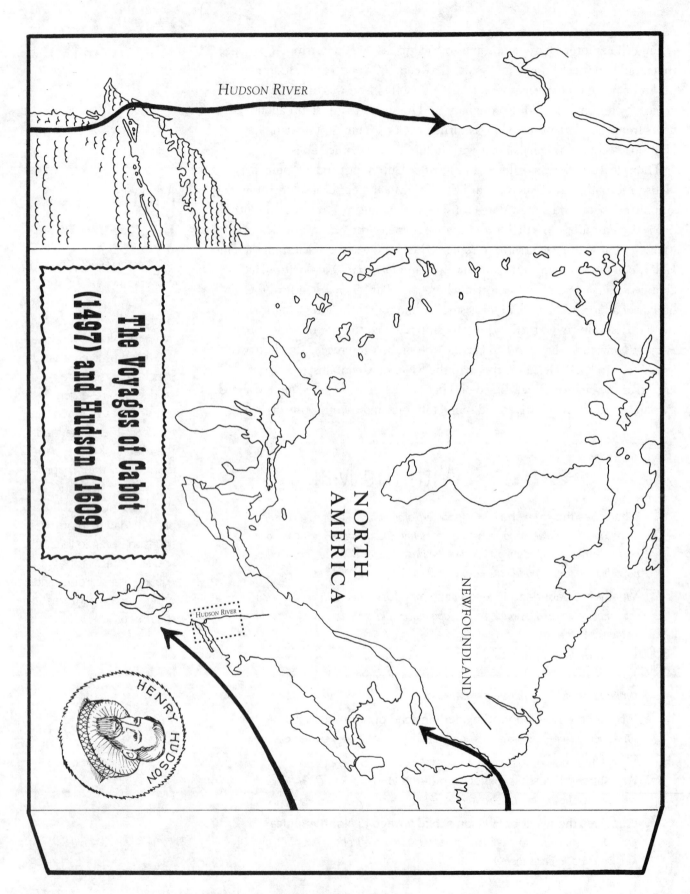

HUDSON RIVER

The Voyages of Cabot (1497) and Hudson (1609)

NORTH AMERICA

NEWFOUNDLAND

HUDSON RIVER

HENRY HUDSON

Interactive 3-D Maps: American History Scholastic Teaching Resources

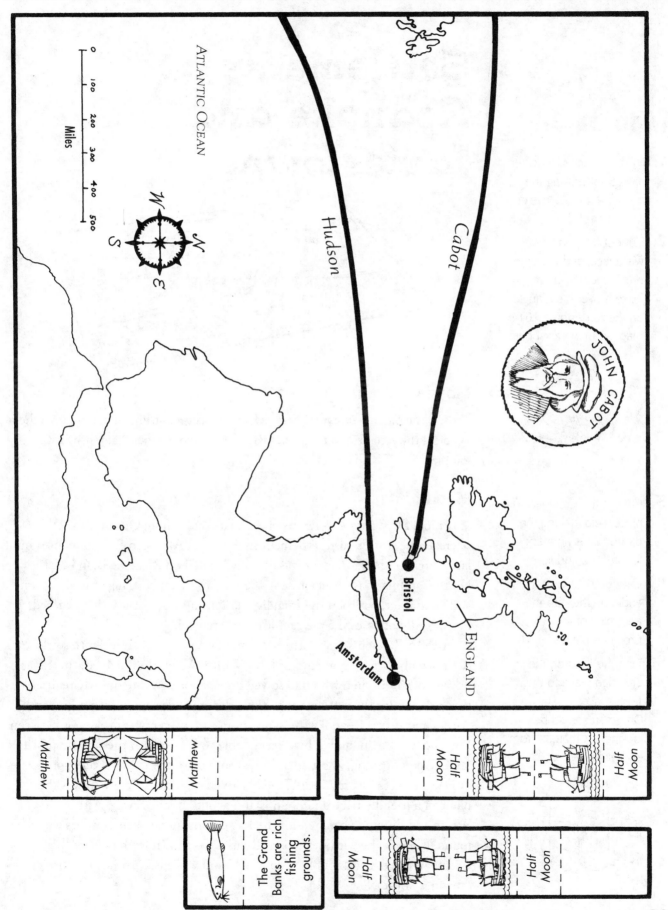

ATLANTIC OCEAN

0
100
200
300
400
500

Miles

N
W — E
S

Hudson

Cabot

JOHN CABOT

Bristol

Amsterdam

ENGLAND

Matthew

Matthew

Half Moon

Half Moon

The Grand Banks are rich fishing grounds.

Half Moon

Half Moon

Interactive 3-D Maps: American History   Scholastic Teaching Resources

29

Mapmaking

1. Follow the instructions on page 5 for making the map, the moving pieces, and other pieces.

2. Cut out the Fort James wall piece, and tape the ends together. Then place it over the triangle on the Jamestown 1614 map, and tape as shown.

3. Cut out the Croatoan piece. Fold it along the dashed lines and tape to form a cylinder.

4. Cut out the two men and tape them to the end folds of the Croatoan piece.

5. Tape the flaps on the Croatoan piece to the TAPE spaces as shown. One man should be looking at Croatoan from each side.

Settlements at Roanoke and Jamestown

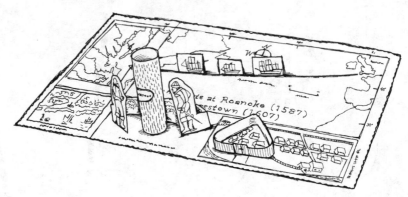

Map in Motion

Insert the *Susan Constant*, *Godspeed*, and *Discovery* at England and move them across the Atlantic to the James River in Virginia, where Jamestown was founded.

Map Points

In 1585, Sir Walter Raleigh received a land grant from Queen Elizabeth I to create the first English settlement in America. Although Raleigh named his land Virginia, the settlement was actually located on Roanoke Island off the North Carolina coast. Raleigh sent 108 men to Roanoke. They stayed a year and built a fort, but then the friendly relationship with local Indians turned hostile. All but 15 of the men returned to England.

In 1587, Raleigh sent another 150 men, women, and children to settle Roanoke under the command of John White. When they arrived, there was no sign of the 15 men who had stayed on Roanoke. White quickly realized that in order for the settlement to flourish it needed supplies from England. After a month on Roanoke, he sailed home. However, war broke out between England and Spain, and White wasn't able to return with the supplies until 1590. Upon arriving, White discovered that all of the settlers were gone. The only clue was the word *CROATOAN* carved on a tree. Croatoan was the name of a friendly tribe and of an island about 50 miles away. Although White and his crew searched for the lost colony, none of the settlers was ever found. (One of the earliest maps of Roanoke is shown to the left of the Croatoan piece. It was published in 1590 and was based on John White's drawings of the New World.)

In 1606, King James I granted the Virginia Company of London the right to found a settlement in Virginia. In December of that year, three ships—the *Susan Constant*, the *Godspeed*, and the *Discovery*—sailed from England with 108 men and boys and 39 sailors aboard. In May 1607, the ships reached Virginia and sailed up a river, which was given the name James. The settlers selected a site on which to build a triangular-shaped fort, which they also named James. Inside the fort's walls, they built houses, a church, and a storehouse. The settlers claimed the land in the name of King James I. To further honor him, they called their settlement Jamestown.

The first few months at Jamestown were extremely difficult. More than half of the men died from malaria, starvation, or Indian attacks. Soon, however, more settlers arrived. Under Captain John Smith's leadership, everyone in the settlement worked hard to ensure Jamestown's success as the first permanent English settlement in America. However, without the help of Chief Powhatan and his confederacy of tribes, Jamestown would have failed. The Indians traded food for English goods. They also taught the settlers how to plant corn and other crops and how to hunt game in the woods. According to legend, Chief Powhatan's daughter, Pocahontas, once saved John Smith's life. Pocahontas married John Rolfe, one of the first English settlers to raise tobacco, and returned with him to England, where she died of pneumonia at the age of 22.

More Map Work

Challenge students to research Chief Powhatan and his confederacy. Then guide them in finding the location of each tribe in the confederacy. Explain that this information usually came from English settlers, such as John Smith, who recorded details about the Native Americans. (To see Smith's map of the Powhatan Confederacy, go to the following Web site: http://www.virginiaplaces. org/nativeamerican/ anglopowhatan.html) Have students write the tribal names in the appropriate areas on their maps. Also ask groups of students to find out more about different aspects of the Powhatan Confederacy, such as government and politics, culture, daily life, relationships with the Europeans, and so on.

Teaching With the Map

1. **What does the map show?** *(It shows the route taken by the three ships carrying settlers who founded the first permanent settlement at Jamestown.)*

2. **Where did the English first try to settle?** *(The first attempt was made on Roanoke Island off the coast of present-day North Carolina.)*

3. **What was *Croatoan*?** *(This word, carved on a tree, was the only clue about what might have happened to the settlers. It might have referred to a tribe of Indians or a nearby island.)*

4. **What was the Virginia Company of London?** *(It was a company that was granted the right by King James I to found a permanent settlement in Virginia.)*

5. **What was Fort James?** *(The triangular fort built by the settlers when they founded Jamestown.)*

6. **How did Powhatan and his people help the Jamestown settlers?** *(They taught them how to grow food and hunt.)*

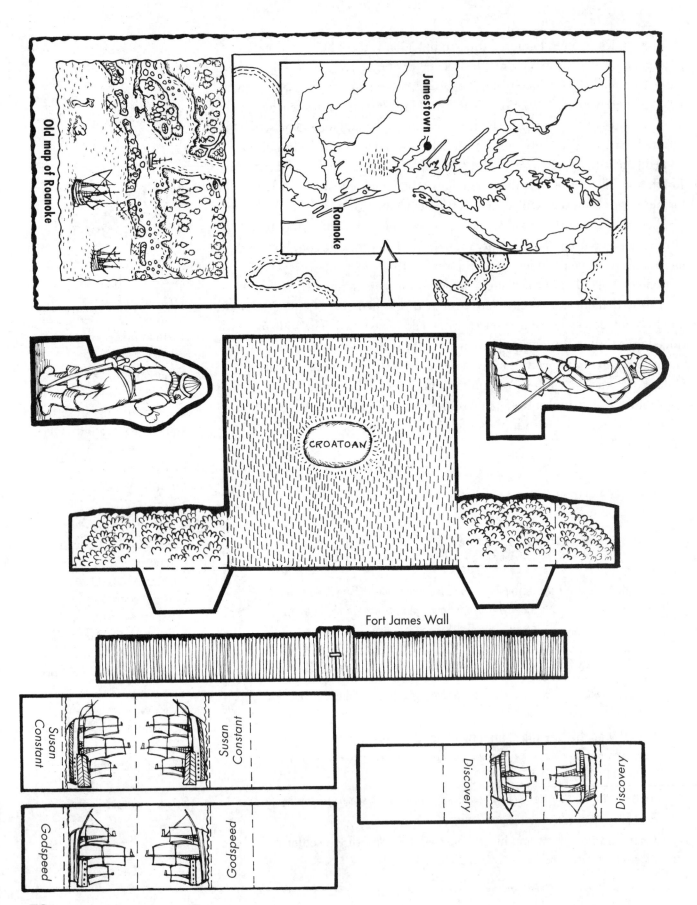

Old map of Roanoke

Jamestown

Roanoke

CROATOAN

Fort James Wall

Susan Constant

Susan Constant

Godspeed

Godspeed

Discovery

Discovery

Interactive 3-D Maps: American History Scholastic Teaching Resources

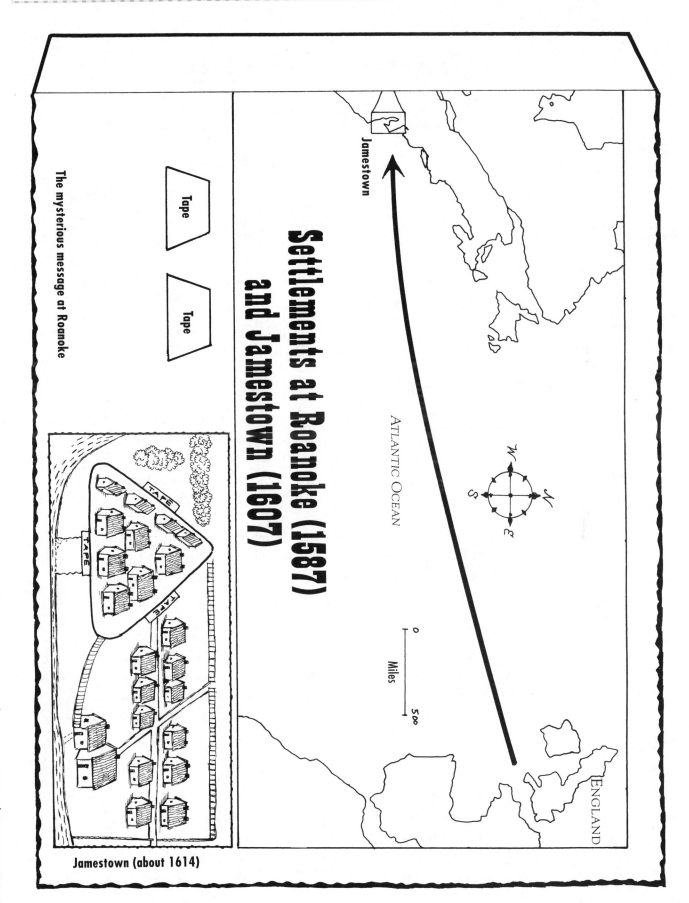

The mysterious message at Roanoke

Tape

Tape

Settlements at Roanoke (1587) and Jamestown (1607)

Jamestown

ATLANTIC OCEAN

Miles
0
500

ENGLAND

Jamestown (about 1614)

TAPE

Voyage of the Mayflower

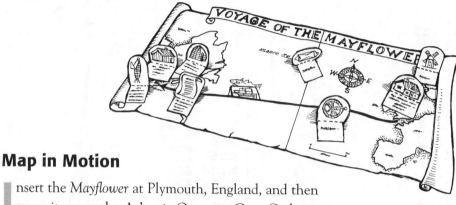

Mapmaking

1. Follow the instructions on page 5 for making the map, the moving piece, and other pieces.

2. Tape the other pieces on the map as follows:
   - the Scrooby piece on England
   - the windmill on Holland
   - the hourglass and astrolabe near the compass rose
   - the Mayflower Compact under the ship's route near Massachusetts
   - the thatched house at the tip of the arrow
   - the wetu and corn pieces near the thatched house

Map in Motion

Insert the *Mayflower* at Plymouth, England, and then move it across the Atlantic Ocean to Cape Cod.

Map Points

The people who we today call the Pilgrims originally lived in and around the rural town of Scrooby, England. When King James I ordered them to live and worship as members of the Church of England, they refused because they felt the church's teachings and ceremonies violated their religious beliefs. Instead, they chose to separate from the Church of England. They were called the Separatists.

To escape persecution for their beliefs, a group of Separatists moved to Holland and settled in the industrial city of Leyden. After 12 years of city life, Separatist parents realized how strongly Dutch ways were influencing their children. They decided to return to England rather than risk their children drifting from their religious beliefs.

In England, they found investors willing to sponsor them on a voyage to America. The Separatists were certain they could practice their religion as they wished in a new land. Since King James I had granted a charter to the Virginia Company of London to settle land up to the 41° N latitude, the Separatists agreed to make their new home within that boundary, specifically in the region around the Hudson River.

On August 15, 1620, a group of Separatists left Plymouth, England, aboard two chartered ships, the *Speedwell* and the *Mayflower*. Unfortunately, the *Speedwell* leaked, and the ships returned to Plymouth. On September 6, only the *Mayflower* took to sea. Aboard were 102 settlers, about half of whom were Separatist men, women, and children. The *Mayflower* was about 90 feet long. The passengers were crowded in a small space below deck with a ceiling so low that many adults had to walk bent over. The air was cold and damp, rain seeped into cracks, there were no bathrooms, and rough seas made many people seasick. In spite of the harsh conditions, only one man died at sea.

The crew of the *Mayflower* relied on an astrolabe and hourglass to keep on course and measure time. About halfway across the Atlantic, the ship encountered a series of storms. High winds, rough waves, and heavy rains damaged the *Mayflower*, forcing it to turn north to escape destruction. Instead of sailing toward New York Harbor, the ship made its way to the tip of Cape Cod.

Realizing that their ship might make landfall outside of the Virginia Company's charter boundary—and therefore out of King James's control—the men wrote an agreement to govern themselves. Almost all of the men signed it. That document, known as the Mayflower Compact and dated November 11, 1620, became North America's first written constitution.

On November 16, an exploring party from the *Mayflower* landed where Provincetown is today. Then, on December 20, the colonists founded a settlement that they called Plymouth Plantation across Cape Cod Bay. There, they built thatched wooden houses. They also met friendly Wampanoag Indians who lived in round, single-family houses called *wetus*. The Wampanoag taught the colonists how to plant corn and other crops, hunt animals in the woods, fish for cod, and gather quahog clams.

Teaching With the Map

1. **What does the map show?** (*The map shows the route of the* Mayflower *from Plymouth, England, to Cape Cod.*)

2. **Who were the Pilgrims?** (*The Pilgrims were a religious group that separated from the Church of England.*)

3. **Why did the Pilgrims move to Holland?** (*They wanted to escape religious persecution.*)

4. **Why did the Pilgrims decide to move to America?** (*After leaving Holland, the Pilgrims concluded that in America they would be free to practice their religion as they wished.*)

5. **What was the Mayflower Compact? Why was it created?** (*It was a self-governing agreement drawn up and signed by the men aboard the Mayflower. Because they were landing outside the area of King James's control, the colonists realized they would need to govern themselves.*)

6. **What was Plymouth Plantation?** (*The settlement erected by the Pilgrims across Cape Cod Bay*)

7. **Who were the Wampanoags?** (*Native Americans who helped the Pilgrims survive at Plymouth Plantation*)

More Map Work

Challenge students to find Scrooby, England, and Leyden, Netherlands, and add these places to their maps. Have them draw arrows to indicate the movements of the Separatists prior to their sailing to America. As an extension, ask students to research Plymouth Plantation and the Wampanoag people. Have them draw the building erected by the colonists and a wetu. They may scale down their drawings to include on their maps.

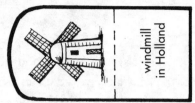

Mayflower

Mayflower

windmill in Holland

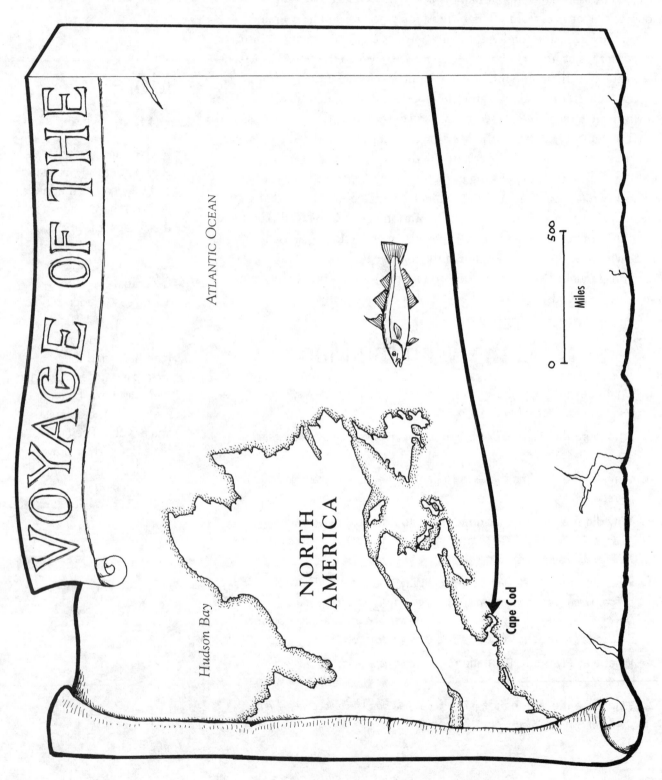

VOYAGE OF THE

ATLANTIC OCEAN

NORTH AMERICA

Hudson Bay

Cape Cod

Miles

0 500

Interactive 3-D Maps: American History   Scholastic Teaching Resources

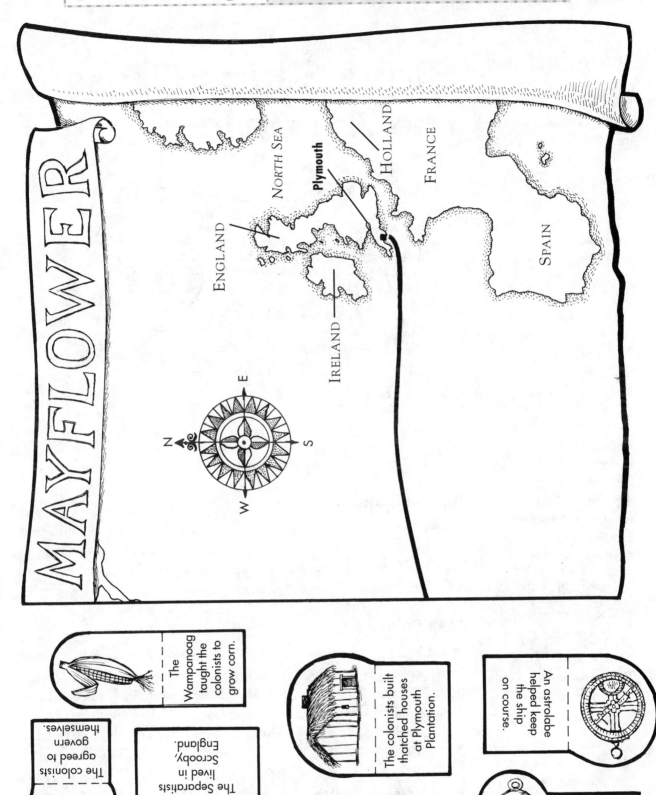

MAYFLOWER

NORTH SEA

ENGLAND

IRELAND

Plymouth

HOLLAND

FRANCE

SPAIN

The Wampanoag taught the colonists to grow corn.

The colonists agreed to govern themselves.

The Separatists lived in Scrooby, England.

The colonists built thatched houses at Plymouth Plantation.

The Wampanoag lived in round houses called wetus.

An astrolabe helped keep the ship on course.

Sailors kept time with an hourglass.

Mapmaking

1. Follow the instructions on page 5 for making the map, the moving piece, and other pieces.

2. Cut out the ship and fold along the dashed lines. Tape the bows together. Then tape the bottom tab inside the ship, as shown.

3. Place the ship on the ship's hold illustration. Tape the back side of the ship to the map, as shown. Lift the ship to reveal the conditions inside the hold.

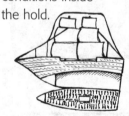

4. Tape the other pieces on the map as follows:

   • people and gold on Africa

   • people, molasses, sugarcane on the West Indies

   • tobacco, grain, fish, fur on the colonies

   • manufactured goods on Europe

Slave Ships Cross the Atlantic

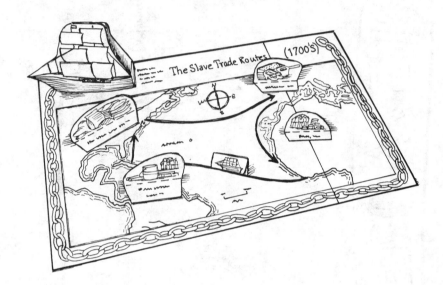

Map in Motion

Insert a ship at the northeast American colonies and then move it to Europe. Then reinsert the ship on the route to Africa and move it toward that continent. Repeat the process from Africa to the West Indies, and from the West Indies to the southeast American colonies.

Map Points

In the 15th century, Portuguese ships sailing from Africa's west coast returned to Europe with Africans they had captured to serve as slaves. By the end of the 17th century, tens of thousands of enslaved Africans had been bought by sugar-plantation owners in Barbados and Jamaica in the West Indies.

The first Africans were brought to Jamestown in 1619 aboard a Dutch ship. About 20 Africans were sold to the colonists as *indentured servants*. An indentured servant had to work for a specified number of years before gaining his or her freedom and receiving land. Over the next few decades, as the colonial agricultural economy grew, growers realized that even though enslaved Africans cost two to three times as much as indentured servants, the Africans could be forced to work for life and thus were a sound economic investment. By the end of the 17th century, more than 28,000 Africans had been enslaved in the American colonies, mostly on farms and plantations.

The trade in slaves formed part of a complex network of trade across the Atlantic Ocean. This network involved the 13 American colonies, Europe, Africa, and the West Indies. The colonies traded tobacco, rice, and other raw materials for manufactured goods from England and the rest of Europe. Merchants in Europe sent firearms, cloth and other manufactured goods, and money to Africa, where slavers traded people and gold for the goods and money. Enslaved Africans were transported across the Atlantic to the West Indies, where they were sold for profit and for sugarcane and other raw materials. Then ships carried the sugarcane and raw materials to the American colonies to be turned into produce goods that could be shipped to England and Europe. Ships also carried enslaved people north from the West Indies directly to the American colonies, where they were sold to farmers and plantation owners. However, most enslaved people were shipped west and south to Latin America.

People in Africa were captured by other Africans, who often were aided by Europeans. The people who had been captured were put in chains and then forced to march hundreds of miles to be branded and sold to slavers. In the brutal voyage from Africa, people were packed into the ship's dark hold so tightly that they had to sleep sitting up. They often were beaten and given little food. Many died of sickness or injuries; others committed suicide. Between the 15th century and just after the United States Civil War in 1865, about 10 million people were forcibly taken from Africa to Europe and the Americas.

More Map Work

Challenge students to research what happened to the Africans aboard the slave ship *Amistad* or the *Henrietta Marie*. Have them draw the route of the ship on their maps and report on what happened to the people on board.

Teaching With the Map

1. **What does the map show?** (*It shows the web of trade routes that included the transportation of enslaved people from Africa to America.*)

2. **Why did the colonists purchase slaves?** (*They needed labor on farms and plantations. Enslaved Africans could be forced to work for life.*)

3. **How did the slave trade work?** (*Enslaved people were traded for raw materials. These raw materials were traded for manufactured goods. Then the manufactured goods were traded for more enslaved people.*)

4. **Where were most Africans sent after they arrived in the West Indies?** (*Although many were sent to the American colonies and then the United States, most were sent to Latin America.*)

5. **What were conditions like aboard a slave ship?** (*Conditions were terrible. People were crowded into a small space. They often were beaten and had little food. Many died on the voyage.*)

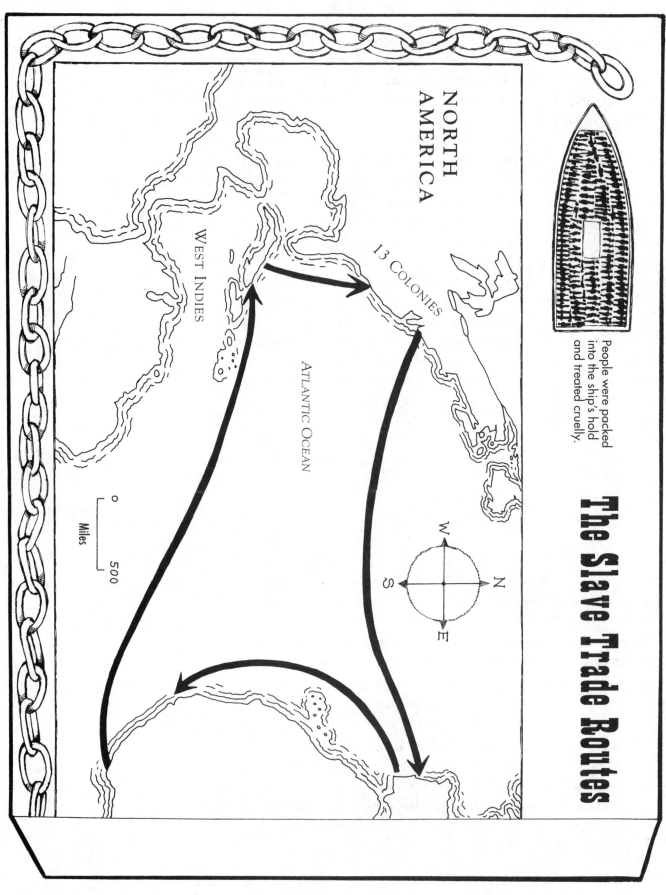

NORTH AMERICA

WEST INDIES

13 COLONIES

ATLANTIC OCEAN

Miles

0   500

People were packed into the ship's hold and treated cruelly.

The Slave Trade Routes

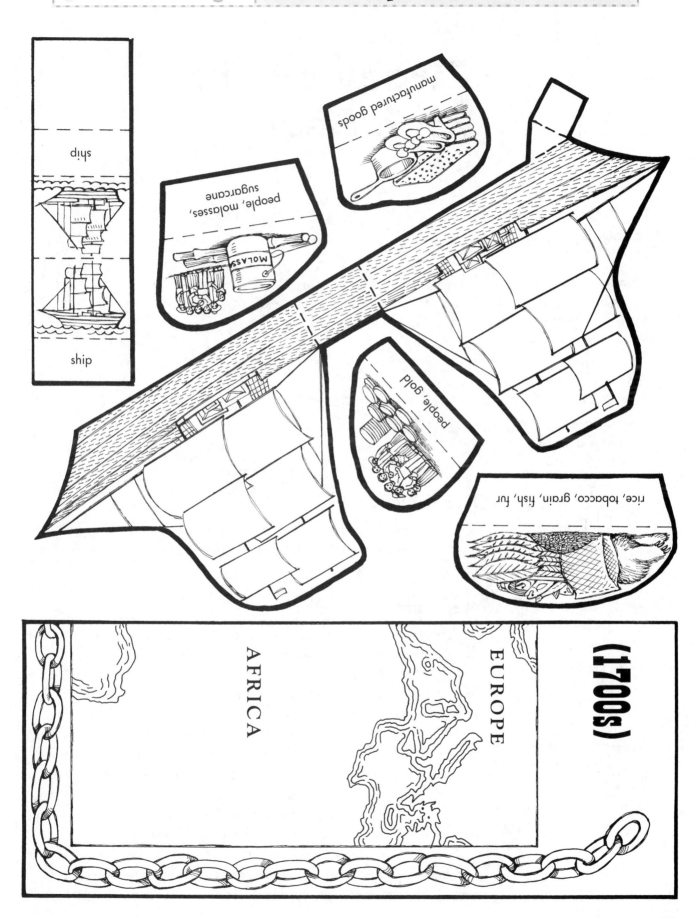

ship

ship

manufactured goods

people, molasses, sugarcane

MOLASS

people, gold

rice, tobacco, grain, fish, fur

AFRICA

EUROPE

(1700s)

Piracy on the High Seas

Mapmaking

1. Follow the instructions on page 5 for making the map and the moving pieces.

2. Cut out the large pirate ship and fold along the dashed lines.

3. Tape the bows together and then fold the flap inside the ship, as shown.

4. Tape the ship on top of its outline to the right of the map.

5. Cut out the skull-and-crossbones flag and fold along the dashed lines.

6. Tape the opened base flaps of the flagpole in place above the pirate ship to the right side of the map.

Map in Motion

Insert the merchant ship at England and move it toward the West Indies. Then insert the pirate ship at the southeastern American colonies and move it to intercept the merchant ship.

Map Points

Pirates roamed the seas and attacked ships long before Europeans settled in America. Pirates were after one thing—wealth. They were loyal to no country. Along with pirates, there were privateers who sailed with the blessing of their government. Their job was to attack and loot as many enemy ships as they could in times of war.

Piracy in America first took hold in the Caribbean. It became known as *buccaneering*. Buccaneers had no home port; rather, they kept sailing from place to place, robbing and looting ships and towns. They found crew members among escaped prisoners and slaves, unhappy sailors and soldiers, and others eager to live a life of adventure. Each crew elected a captain, and each pirate shared in an equal part of the haul. However, the captain, surgeon, and gunner usually rewarded themselves with extra shares as bonuses.

Pirates rarely harmed the passengers and crews aboard the ships they robbed. They were after goods and coins such as silver *pieces of eight*. Pieces of eight were Spanish coins that were the main currency both in Latin America and in the 13 colonies. Sometimes the mere sight of a pirate ship's skull-and-crossbones flag was enough to make a merchant ship surrender without a fight. This was ideal for the pirates for they didn't have to engage in battle.

By raiding Spanish ships and ports in America, pirates aided the French and English in their undeclared war against Spain. From about 1650 to 1720, pirate activity expanded from the Caribbean to the 13 American colonies. The English sea captain Edward Teach, whom colonists feared as the notorious Bluebeard, robbed ships from the coast of Virginia to the Carolinas. Both colonial governments and the British parliament passed laws making piracy a crime punishable by death. However, because pirates paid for food and supplies with pieces of eight, they were welcomed in cities and towns up and down the coast.

Although women were not allowed on pirate ships, not all pirates were men. Mary Read disguised herself in sailor's clothes and was captured aboard her ship by the pirate John Rackham, also known as Calico Jack. Mary then turned pirate herself.

In the early 1700s, the British Royal Navy made a concerted effort to seek out and crush pirate activities along the coast of the colonies. Many pirates were hanged, but those who escaped returned to the safety of the Caribbean and continued their acts of piracy.

More Map Work

Jean Laffite was a pirate who fought with Andrew Jackson in the Battle of New Orleans. He also spent time in Galveston, Texas, which was a hot spot for pirates. Challenge students to research Laffite, and draw a map showing his exploits. As an extension, guide students in exploring the Jolly Roger and other pirate flags. (You might visit the Pirates! Facts and Legends Web site at http://www.piratesinfo.com) Students can make and place the flags on their maps in the region where each pirate sailed.

Teaching With the Map

1. **What does the map show?** (The map shows a pirate ship intercepting a merchant vessel in order to rob it.)

2. **Who were buccaneers?** (Buccaneers were pirates who had no home ports and who sailed in the Caribbean.)

3. **What are pieces of eight?** (They are Spanish coins that were used as the main currency in both Latin America and the 13 colonies.)

4. **Why were pirates and their activities welcomed by some governments and some coastal cities?** (By raiding Spanish ships, pirates helped England and France in their undeclared war against Spanish interests in America. Cities and towns welcomed pirate money spent on food and supplies.)

5. **What happened to the pirates in the early 1700s?** (The British Royal Navy captured and hanged many pirates. Other pirates returned to the Caribbean and continued their activities.)

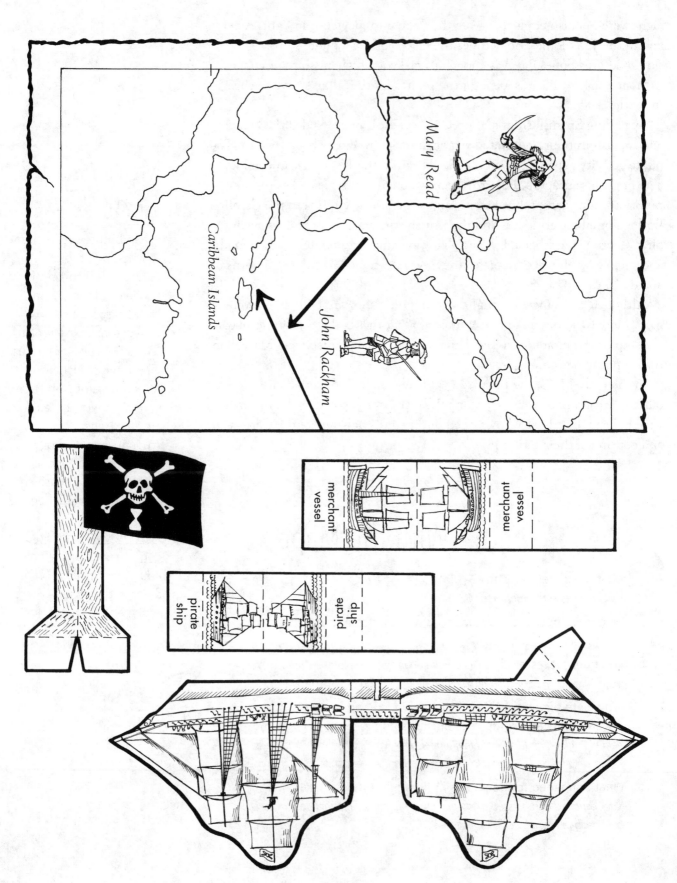

Mary Read

Caribbean Islands

John Rackham

merchant vessel

merchant vessel

pirate ship

pirate ship

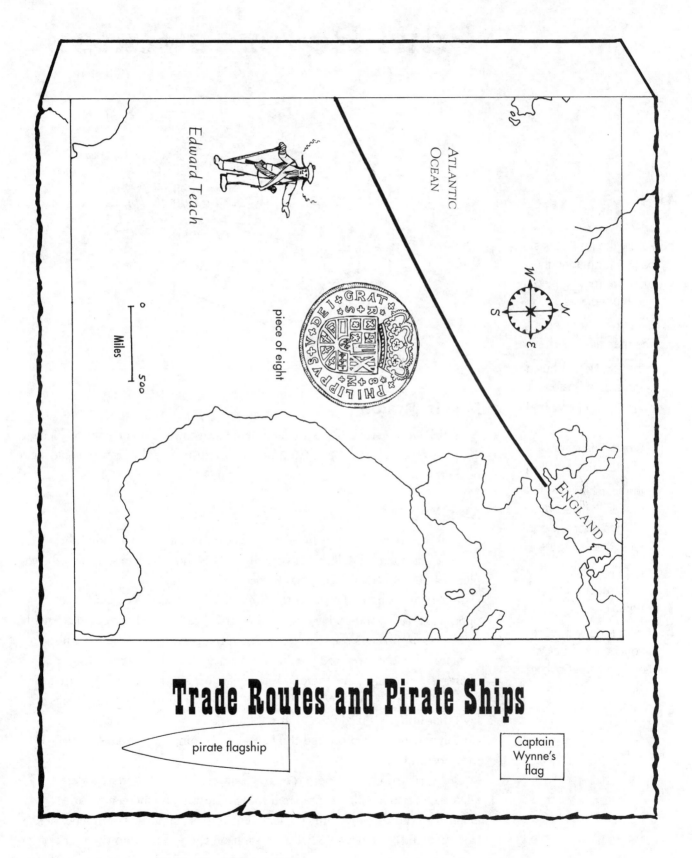

Edward Teach

ATLANTIC
OCEAN

piece of eight

Miles

0

500

ENGLAND

Trade Routes and Pirate Ships

pirate flagship

Captain
Wynne's
flag

Interactive 3-D Maps: American History   Scholastic Teaching Resources

Paul Revere's Ride

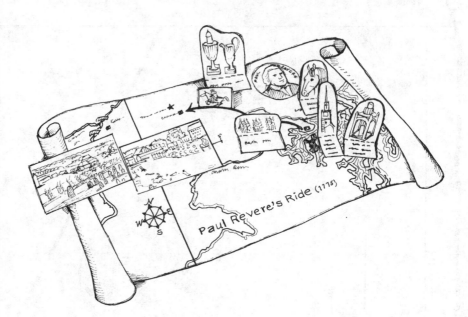

Paul Revere's Ride (1775)

Mapmaking

1. Follow the instructions on page 5 for making the map, the moving piece, and other pieces.

2. Tape the other pieces on the map as follows:
   - the Old North Church steeple on Boston and the lantern piece next to it
   - Brown Beauty on Charlestown
   - the marching British soldiers between the Charles River and Paul Revere's route
   - the silversmith piece near Paul Revere's portrait

3. Cut out the two scenes and tape them below Lexington and Concord.

Map in Motion

Insert Paul Revere on Brown Beauty in Charlestown. Then move the piece to Lexington to show his ride warning the colonists that the British would soon be on the march.

Map Points

Paul Revere was born in 1734 and grew up in Boston. As an adult, he became a master colonial silversmith. In his shop, Revere sold silver bowls, plates, and other home items that he designed and made.

Revere also was a member of the Sons of Liberty, a secret group that opposed British policies. He engraved political cartoons that depicted British rule as tyrannical. As the conflict between the patriots and the British escalated, Revere often rode to and from Boston and the surrounding countryside to deliver messages to other patriots and to return with their responses. During the 1760s, when the British Parliament passed a series of laws that unfairly taxed the colonists, Paul Revere was one of a group of Boston patriots who protested the taxes by dumping shiploads of British tea into Boston Harbor.

On April 16, 1775, Revere rode to Concord, Massachusetts, to alert *militiamen* (citizen soldiers prepared to fight during an emergency) and *minutemen* (militia regiments made up entirely of supporters of independence from England) of a possible British assault on them. Then, on the night of April 18, Revere rode to warn patriot leaders John Hancock and Samuel

Adams that the British soldiers (also known as *redcoats*) knew they were hiding in Lexington and would soon be there to capture them. What Revere didn't know was whether the redcoats were coming by land or by water. He arranged for a lookout to hang one lantern in the steeple of Boston's Old North Church if British troops were marching by land and two lanterns if they were first crossing the Charles River. Revere waited for the signal in a rowboat on the Charles River. When he saw two lanterns, he rowed from Boston to Charlestown, borrowed a fast horse named Brown Beauty, and rode toward Lexington. Along the way, Revere alerted farmers and townspeople that the redcoats were coming and it was time to take arms.

Revere reached Lexington in time to warn Adams and Hancock, and they fled safely. There, Revere was joined by Samuel Prescott and William Dawes, who rode with him toward Concord to spread the alarm. When the three horsemen were stopped by a British patrol, Dawes and Prescott escaped to Concord, but Revere was held. However, he tricked the British into letting him go, albeit without his horse, by making them believe that they were the ones about to be attacked by mobs of angry colonists. Revere returned to Lexington, where he witnessed the start of the American Revolution the next morning.

Teaching With the Map

1. **What does the map show?** *(It shows Paul Revere's ride on April 18, 1775, to warn patriot leaders, farmers, and townspeople that the British soldiers were on their way.)*

2. **Who was Paul Revere?** *(He was an American patriot and a master colonial silversmith.)*

3. **Who was Paul Revere trying to save on the night of April 18, 1775, and why?** *(The patriot leaders John Hancock and Samuel Adams, who were about to be captured by the British)*

4. **What was Paul Revere waiting for in the rowboat?** *(He was waiting for a signal from a lookout in the North Church steeple that would tell him how the redcoats were coming.)*

5. **What happened when Revere reached Charlestown?** *(He borrowed a horse and set off for Lexington.)*

6. **What happened to prevent Paul Revere from reaching Concord? Who alerted the people of Concord?** *(He was stopped by a British patrol. Samuel Prescott and William Dawes, who had joined Revere, managed to escape and rode on to Concord.)*

More Map Work

Ask students to research and show the route the British soldiers took on their maps. They may use dashed lines to indicate the route. Then, challenge them to complete either of the following projects:

- Ask students to indicate the route of the British retreat following the battles of Lexington and Concord with dotted lines. If they wish to include patriot attacks on the retreating troops, they can draw stars.

- Challenge students to plan a land route to Concord for the British soldiers. Remind them to use different markings to show this route on their maps. Then, ask them to explain which route they think would have been better for the British to take—land or sea.

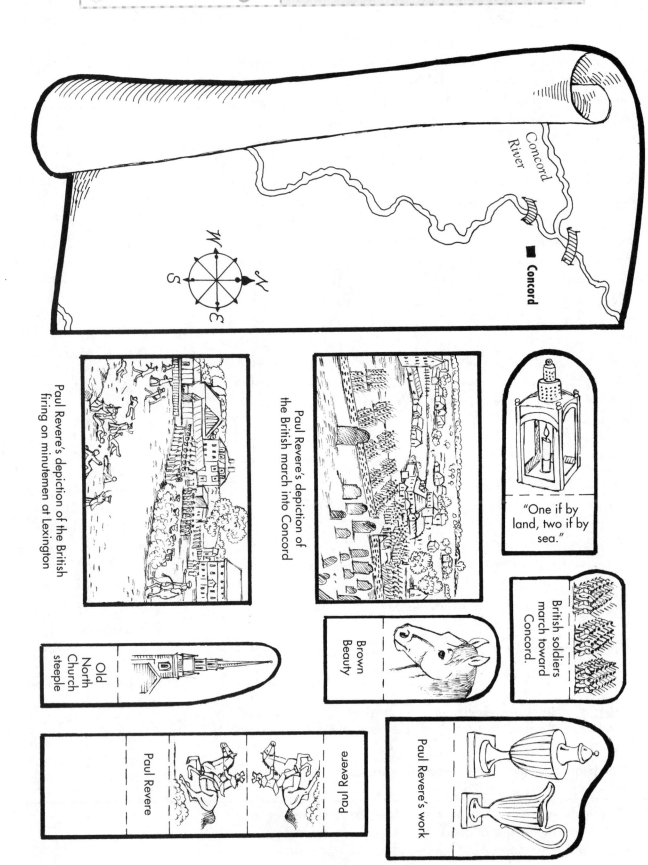

Concord River

■ **Concord**

Paul Revere's depiction of the British firing on minutemen at Lexington

Paul Revere's depiction of the British march into Concord

"One if by land, two if by sea."

British soldiers march toward Concord.

Old North Church steeple

Brown Beauty

Paul Revere

Paul Revere

Paul Revere's work

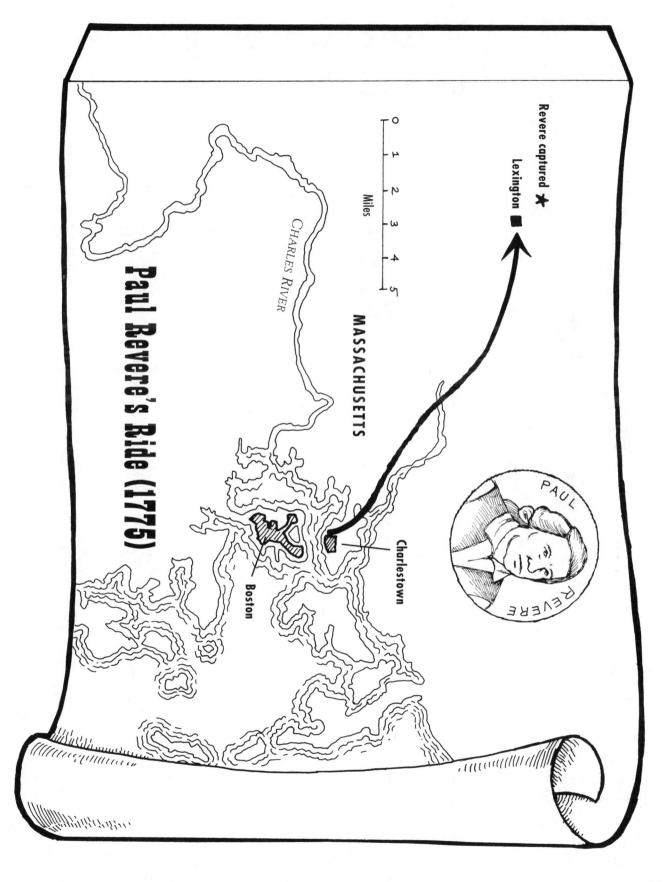

Paul Revere's Ride (1775)

MASSACHUSETTS

CHARLES RIVER

Miles
0 1 2 3 4 5

Revere captured ✶
■ Lexington

Charlestown

Boston

PAUL REVERE

Mapmaking

1. Follow the instructions on page 5 for making the maps, the moving army piece, and other pieces.

Small Map

2. Cut out the three boat pieces and the "TAPE 3 TROOP BOATS HERE" piece.

3. Fold the TAPE piece and tape as shown.

4. Fold the three boats and tape to the TAPE piece, as shown.

5. Insert the piece into the cut-open line, as shown.

Large Map

6. Tape the other pieces to the large map as follows:

   • the Hessian drummer boy and Hessian soldier to the right of Trenton

   • the cannon piece above Princeton

   • Washington above the cut-open arrow

Washington Crosses the Delaware

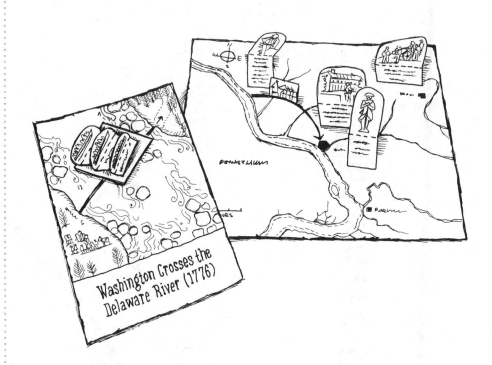

Maps in Motion

On the small map, insert Washington's three-boat piece on the Pennsylvania side of the Delaware River and move them to the New Jersey side. On the large map, insert Washington and his troops on the New Jersey side of the Delaware River and move them to Trenton.

Map Points

By the summer of 1776, American's hopes for victory in the war against England had dimmed. Troops under the command of General George Washington battled the much larger, better-equipped, and better-trained British army led by General William Howe. The several battles that took place between the two sides near New York City in late August resulted in major American defeats. The British advance in the fall forced Washington and his men to retreat south through New Jersey, across the Delaware River, and into Pennsylvania. In their advance, the British took over towns, including Princeton and Trenton in New Jersey. As Christmas approached, Washington decided upon a bold strategy. He commanded less than 8,000 men, and he knew that without a victory many of his troops would return to their homes when their enlistment was up at the end of December. Washington decided to risk everything with a Christmas-night sneak attack on the enemy barracks at Trenton.

On Christmas night, Washington led 2,400 men through a snowstorm to McConkey's Ferry on the Delaware River. It was bitterly cold and rowing across the river was made even more difficult by ice. Once the American troops reformed on the New Jersey side of the river, they marched about 10 miles through the snow until they reached Trenton early in the morning. Trenton was held by a troop of *Hessians*—German soldiers hired for money by the British to increase the strength of their forces. Having eaten and drunk too much at the holiday celebration the day before, most of the Hessians were fast asleep. Victory was swift for Washington and his men. They killed 30 enemy soldiers and captured more than 900 others, along with badly needed cannons and other supplies. Six days later, Washington led his men north to another victory against 1,200 British troops at Princeton, New Jersey.

The Battle of Trenton was a major victory in the Revolutionary War. It demonstrated Washington's gifts as a strategist, leader, and courageous fellow soldier. When hopes were dim, he lifted the spirits of his men. They knew he was there for them, that he was suffering along with them, and that they always could rely on him.

More Map Work

Major battles followed the American victories at Trenton and Princeton. In 1777, there were confrontations at Brandywine, Pennsylvania, and Saratoga and Fort Ticonderoga in New York. Divide the class into groups, and have each group report on a battle by drawing maps of troop movements at each site.

Teaching With the Maps

1. **What do the maps show?** *(The small map shows Washington and his troops rowing across the Delaware River. The large map shows them marching to Trenton to attack the enemy.)*

2. **Why did Washington plan the sneak attack on Trenton?** *(He had suffered numerous defeats at the hands of the British and knew his army would soon fall apart without a victory.)*

3. **What were conditions like on Christmas night?** *(It was stormy and bitterly cold. The Delaware River was full of ice, and there was snow on the ground.)*

4. **Who were the Hessians?** *(Germans hired by the British to fight on their side)*

5. **What happened at Trenton?** *(The Hessians were still asleep from celebrating the holiday and were quickly defeated by Washington's troops.)*

6. **Where was the next battle fought?** *(Washington and his troops marched north to Princeton and defeated the enemy there.)*

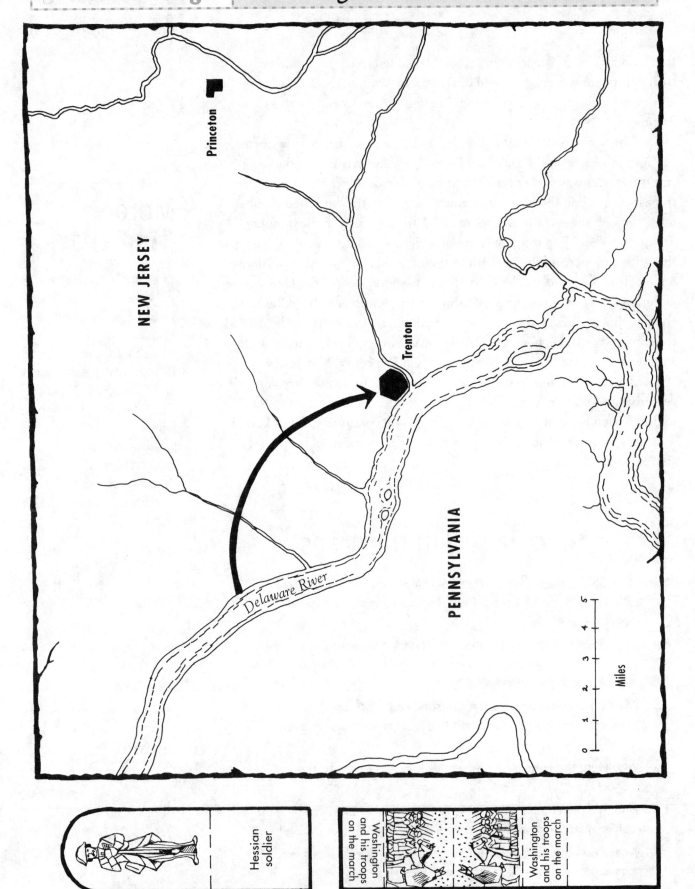

NEW JERSEY

Princeton

Trenton

Delaware River

PENNSYLVANIA

Miles
0 1 2 3 4 5

Hessian
soldier

Washington
and his troops
on the march

Washington
and his troops
on the march

Interactive 3-D Maps: American History   Scholastic Teaching Resources

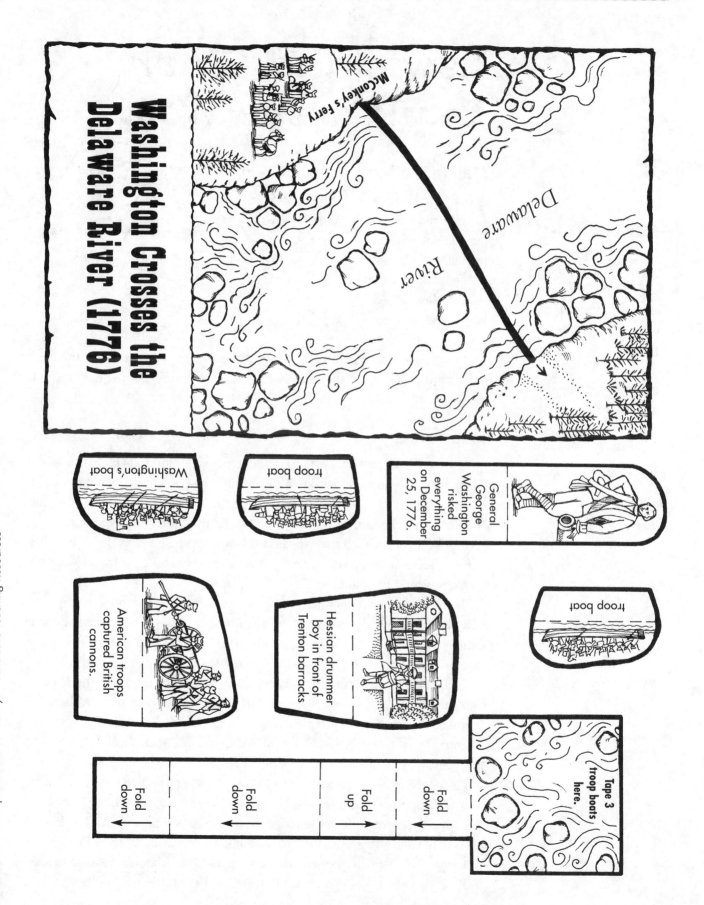

Washington Crosses the Delaware River (1776)

McConkey's Ferry

Delaware River

General George Washington risked everything on December 25, 1776.

Washington's boat

troop boat

troop boat

American troops captured British cannons.

Hessian drummer boy in front of Trenton barracks.

Tape 3 troop boats here.

Fold down

Fold down

Fold up

Fold down

Fold down

Lewis and Clark Explore the West

Map in Motion

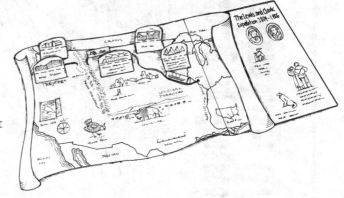

I nsert the keelboat piece and the pirogue side of the pirogue/canoe piece at St. Louis and move it to Fort Mandan. At Fort Mandan, move the keelboat back to St. Louis. From Fort Mandan, move the pirogue to the eastern side of the Rocky Mountains. Then insert the canoe side on the western side of the Rockies and move it to the Pacific Ocean.

Map Points

I n 1803, President Thomas Jefferson sent an expedition to explore the Louisiana Territory, which the United States had purchased from France. He believed a direct and profitable route to the Far East would be found in the West and that the United States would benefit from the wealth of the new territory. Jefferson called the expedition the Corps of Discovery. He named his personal secretary Meriwether Lewis to lead it; Lewis chose his friend William Clark as second-in-command.

With nearly four dozen men, the explorers left St. Louis and sailed up the Missouri River on May 14, 1804, in a keelboat and two flat-bottomed dugouts called *pirogues*. The keelboat, measuring 55 feet long and 8 feet wide, was maneuvered with oars, poles, and, when the wind was favorable, sails. Lewis and Clark kept daily journals of where they went, what they saw, the plants and animals they collected, and the Native Americans they met. In their journals, they described 178 plant species and 122 animal species new to science at that time. The explorers also shipped specimens back to the president—including a live prairie dog.

As the expedition traveled up the Missouri River, the men saw vast herds of buffalo on the Great Plains. They encountered Sioux who lived in tepees and Mandans who built round lodges that formed permanent villages. Lewis and Clark gave gifts to the Indians, including a peace medal from President Jefferson. The expedition members constructed Fort Mandan near a Mandan Indian village. At night, they would sit around campfires while Pierre

Mapmaking

1. Follow the instructions on page 5 for making the map, the moving pieces, and other pieces.

2. Tape each piece on top of its corresponding name on the map.

Cruzatte entertained them with the fiddle. There, they met the fur trader Toussaint Charbonneau and his pregnant wife, Sacagawea. Sacagawea was a Shoshone Indian who had been captured and sold to Charbonneau. Lewis and Clark hired the Charbonneaus as interpreters, and they soon proved to be valuable guides.

Part of the crew turned back at Fort Mandan and returned to St. Louis in the keelboat. The rest continued up the Missouri River in the pirogues and canoes they had built. By the time they reached Shoshone country, Lewis and Clark realized there was no northwest passage to the Far East; to continue, they would have to find a crossing through the Rocky Mountains—and they would need horses. Fortunately, they were able to buy horses from the Shoshones, whose chief was Sacagawea's long-lost brother.

The expedition crossed the Rockies at Lemhi Pass and entered the Oregon Territory. They sailed in canoes on the Snake and Columbia Rivers to the Pacific Ocean. In November 1805, every member of the expedition including Sacagawea and York, Clark's slave, voted to spend the winter in Fort Clatsop, which they had built. On March 23, 1806, the expedition left the fort to return home. From July 3 to August 12, the group separated to explore different areas and then rejoined. They arrived in St. Louis on September 23, 1806, with maps and records detailing their discoveries.

More Map Work

Challenge students to research the return route the expedition took from the Pacific Ocean to St. Louis. Have students use arrows to indicate the route and how the two groups split apart and then reformed.

Teaching With the Map

1. **What does the map show?** *(It shows the route taken by Lewis and Clark's expedition as they explored the Louisiana Territory and parts of the Oregon Territory.)*

2. **Why did Jefferson send the expedition to explore the West?** *(He was certain it would find a northwest passage to the Far East and the new territory's wealth would benefit the United States.)*

3. **Who were Lewis and Clark?** *(Meriwether Lewis was Jefferson's personal secretary assigned to lead the expedition. William Clark, Lewis's friend, was named second-in-command.)*

4. **What did the expedition encounter as they sailed up the Missouri River?** *(They met Native Americans of different tribes, collected specimens of plants and animals unknown to science at the time, saw vast herds of buffalo on the Great Plains.)*

5. **How did Sacagawea help the expedition in Shoshone country?** *(Her long-lost brother was the Shoshone chief, and he allowed the expedition to buy horses so they could cross the Rockies at Lemhi Pass.)*

6. **What did the expedition do when it reached the Pacific Ocean?** *(They built Fort Clatsop and spent the winter there before returning to St. Louis.)*

CANADA

St. Louis

MISSISSIPPI RIVER

Sioux tepees

■ Fort Mandan

Missouri River

Mandan village

prairie dogs

black-footed ferret

LOUISIANA TERRITORY

vast bison herds

250

Miles

0

Chinook houses

Columbia River

Snake River

Lemhi Pass

ROCKY MOUNTAINS

Fort Clatsop

OREGON TERRITORY

prairie chicken

MEXICO

Clark's diary

N

PACIFIC OCEAN

Interactive 3-D Maps: American History Scholastic Teaching Resources

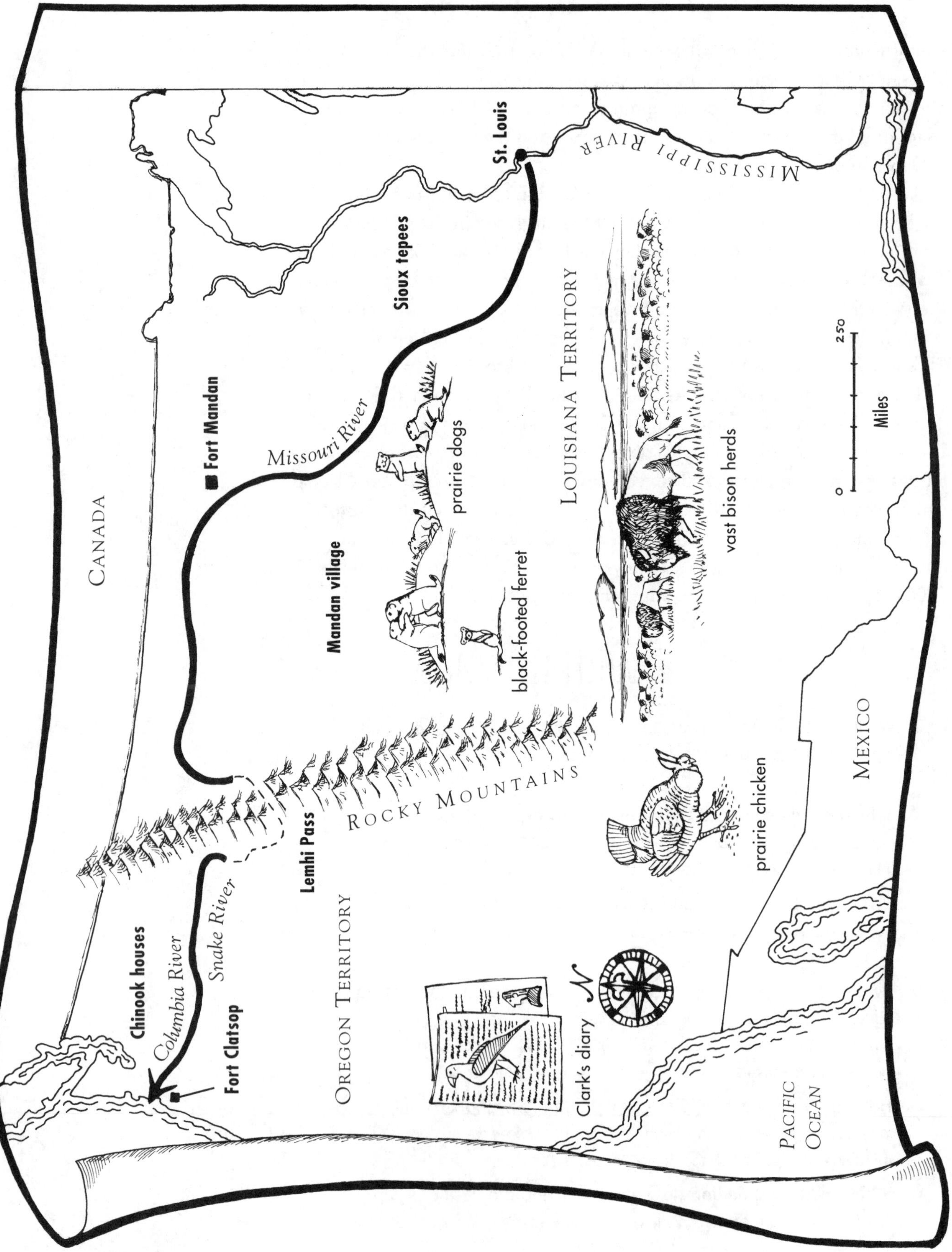

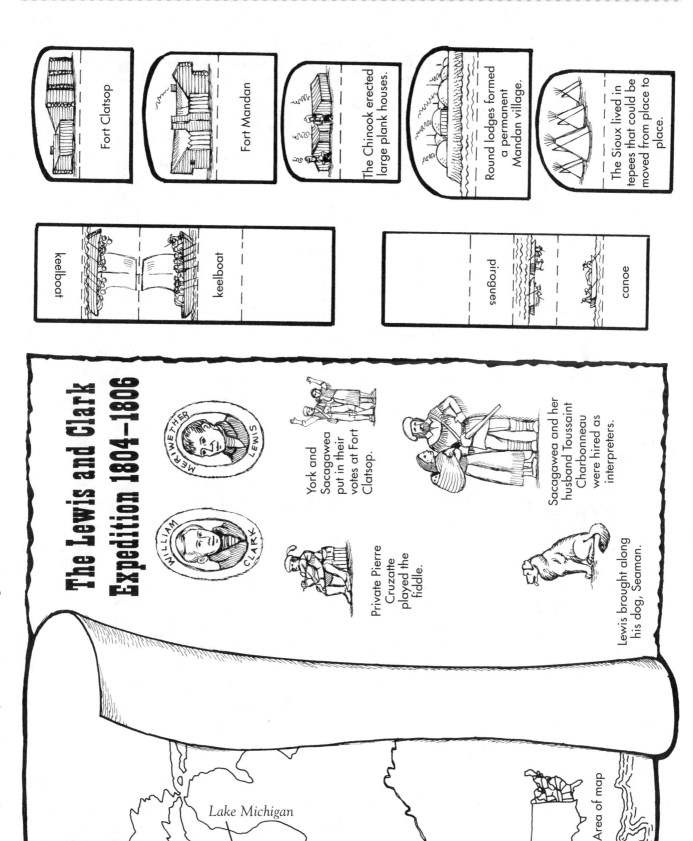

Fort Clatsop

Fort Mandan

The Chinook erected large plank houses.

Round lodges formed a permanent Mandan village.

The Sioux lived in tepees that could be moved from place to place.

keelboat

keelboat

pirogues

canoe

The Lewis and Clark Expedition 1804–1806

MERIWETHER LEWIS

WILLIAM CLARK

York and Sacagawea put in their votes at Fort Clatsop.

Sacagawea and her husband Toussaint Charbonneau were hired as interpreters.

Private Pierre Cruzatte played the fiddle.

Lewis brought along his dog, Seaman.

Lake Michigan

Area of map

A Ride Along the Erie Canal

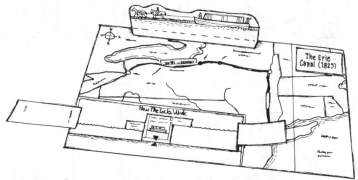

Mapmaking

1. Follow the instructions on page 5 for making the map and the moving pieces.

2. Cut out the large canal-barge piece and fold along the dashed lines. Tape on the map where indicated.

3. Cut out the pull strip and extensions A and B. Tape an extension to each end of the pull strip. Tape both front and back.

4. On the "How the Locks Work" inset, cut open the solid black lines and the boxes labeled "cut out."

5. Slip the pull strip through the cut lines, as shown. Pull the strip until "Step 1" is in the center and the arrows are aligned.

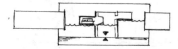

Map in Motion

Insert a steamboat at New York City and move it up the Hudson River to Albany. Then insert a canal barge pulled by horses at Albany and move it along the Erie Canal to Buffalo and Lake Erie. Students can pull an illustrated strip to find out how a lock works.

Map Points

By the early 1800s, the new nation that began as 13 colonies had expanded west of the Appalachian Mountains to the Mississippi River. Settlers needed goods produced in the East, and manufacturers were eager to expand their markets. Western raw materials and food such as grains were in demand in the East. Hauling goods and freight by road was slow, uncertain, and expensive. River travel didn't extend far enough inland.

In 1807, Robert Fulton's *Clermont*, the first American steamboat, sailed up the Hudson River from New York City to Albany. In 1818, a paddleboat was launched on Lake Erie. It carried passengers and goods from Buffalo west to Detroit. However, there was no direct water connection between the Hudson River and Lake Erie. Realizing the enormous economic potential of such a connection across his state, New York governor DeWitt Clinton backed the idea of building a canal between the two bodies of water. With legislative approval, the plan to build a canal in short sections was implemented. As each section was completed, it would be available to local boat traffic.

Over nearly eight years, using horse-drawn plows, scoops, and the labor of immigrants (most of whom were Irish), the 363-mile-long Erie Canal was built. The canal had 83 *locks* (see below for an explanation of how a lock works.) It was 4 feet deep and 40 feet wide. With the completion of the Erie Canal on October 26, 1825, boats could pick up freight in New York City, transport it to Albany, and carry it to Lake Erie and other points west. Each boat, or *barge*, was pulled at about one-and-a-half miles per hour by horses or mules that walked parallel to the canal on *towpaths* that were 10 feet wide. Some barges carried passengers, some of whom were immigrants, while others carried only freight. The Erie Canal proved to be an immediate success. It cut the travel time between the East and the West, moved thousands of tons of freight to and from the West, greatly reduced costs, and helped transform New York City into a major trade center on the East Coast and Buffalo into a major Great Lakes port.

The Erie Canal was built with locks that helped lift boats from lower to higher elevations or lower them in the reverse direction. The total lift between the sea-level Hudson River and Lake Erie was more than 500 feet. Each lock was a section of the waterway that could be closed off with wooden gates. When a boat moving upstream entered a lock, the lower gate opened while the upper gate remained closed (Step 1). Once the boat was inside the lock, the lower gate was closed. Small channels in the upper gate were opened to allow water to flow into the lock (Step 2). As the lock filled, the boat was raised up (Step 3). When the water reached the level of the upper gate, that gate was opened, and the boat passed out of the lock (Step 4). A boat traveling downstream could then enter the lock. When the upper gates were closed, water was drained through channels opened in the lower gates. Today the Erie Canal is still in use as part of the New York State Barge Canal System.

Teaching With the Map

1. **What does the map show?** *(The map shows how the Erie Canal linked the Hudson River to Lake Erie and created a route for passengers and freight from New York City to the West.)*

2. **Why was the Erie Canal built?** *(The canal was built as a cheaper, shorter, and more reliable route for goods and people from the East to the West. It also moved raw materials and foods in the opposite direction.)*

3. **How did barges move along the canal?** *(They were pulled by horses or mules that walked along the towpaths parallel to the canal.)*

4. **What changes occurred as a result of the construction of the Erie Canal?** *(Travel times and freight costs were reduced; New York City and Buffalo became major trade ports.)*

5. **Why were locks necessary?** *(Locks raised or lowered boats as the elevations of the canal increased or decreased.)*

6. **Invite a student to use the pull strip and explain how a lock works. Call on another student to explain the process in the reverse direction.**

More Map Work

Following the success of the Erie Canal, Ohio and Pennsylvania also constructed canal systems. Challenge students to research one of the following canal systems:

- the system of canals that eventually connected eastern waterways with the Mississippi River

- the water route that linked Chicago and the Atlantic Ocean

Have students draw maps to illustrate their findings.

CANADA

Tape canal barge here.

Lake Erie

Buffalo

NEW YORK

Rochester

Erie Canal

Lake Ontario

Syracuse

PENNSYLVANIA

Rome

How the Locks Work

Cut out

Cut out

Align arrows

Miles

0

50

Albany

New York City

Hudson River

VERMONT

Interactive 3-D Maps: American History Scholastic Teaching Resources

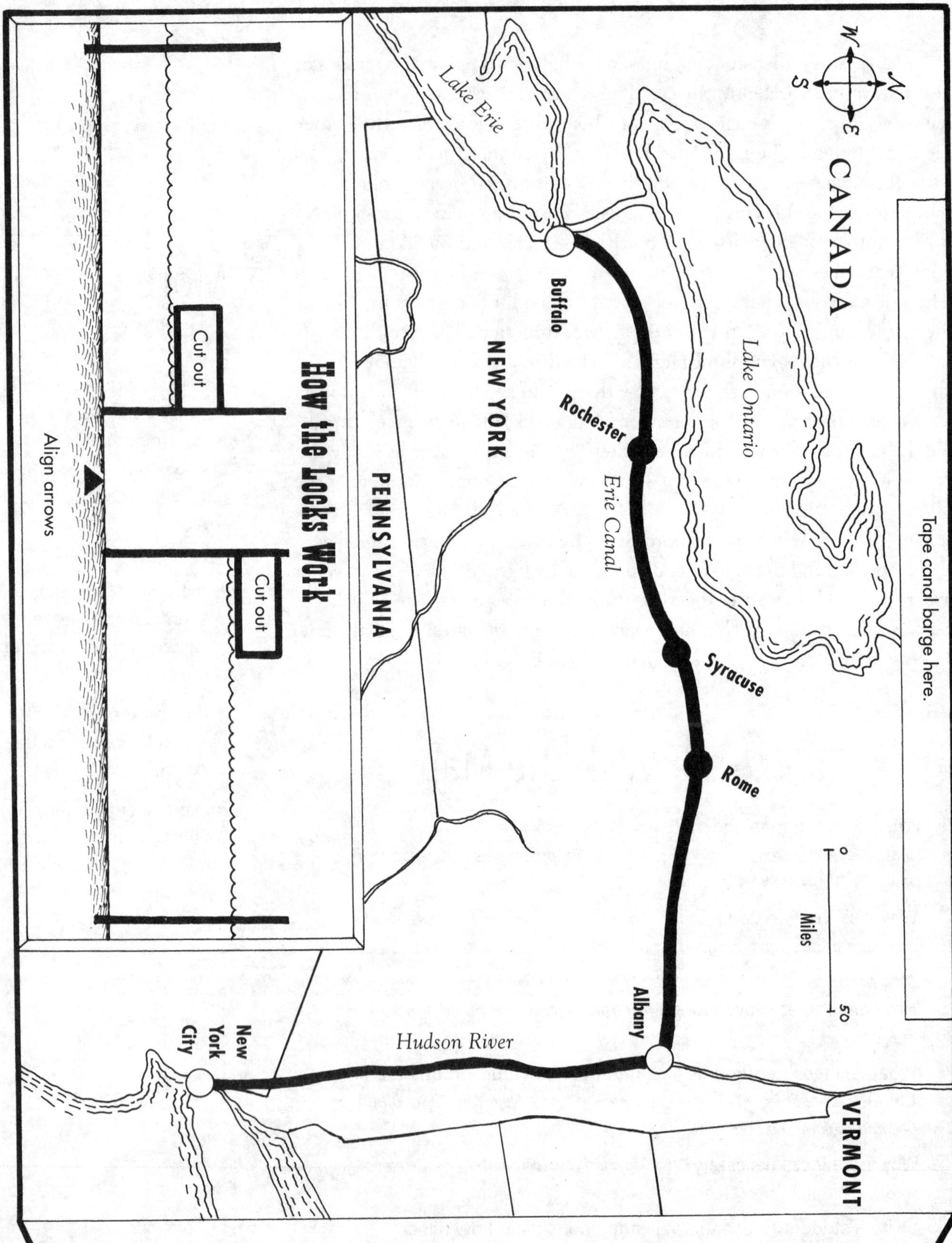

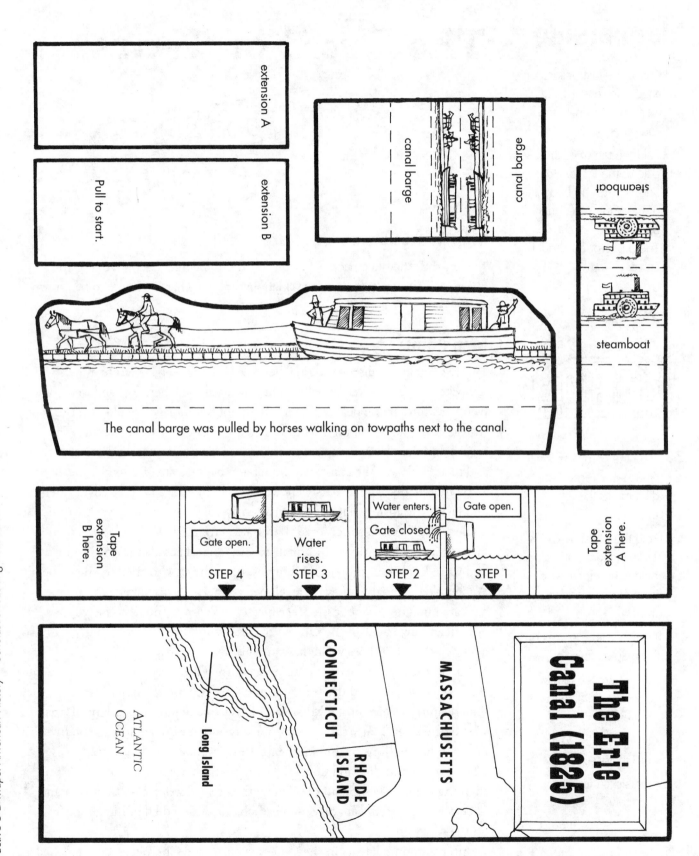

extension A

extension B

Pull to start.

canal barge

canal barge

steamboat

steamboat

The canal barge was pulled by horses walking on towpaths next to the canal.

Tape extension B here.

Gate open.

Water rises.

STEP 3

Water enters.

Gate closed.

STEP 2

Gate open.

STEP 1

Tape extension A here.

STEP 4

CONNECTICUT

MASSACHUSETTS

RHODE ISLAND

ATLANTIC OCEAN

Long Island

The Erie Canal (1825)

Mapmaking

1. Follow the instructions on page 5 for making the map, the moving piece, and other pieces.

2. Fold the tab at each side of the White House and tape to the back side of the Supreme Court background, as shown. The background should curve.

3. Tape the complete White House–Supreme Court diorama to the left of the map.

4. Fold the Marshall and Jackson pieces and tape below the diorama so both pieces stand in front.

5. Tape the other pieces on the map as follows:

   • the Cherokee family above the Trail of Tears in Kentucky

   • the graves below the trail in Missouri

   • the sick in Indian Territory

The Trail of Tears

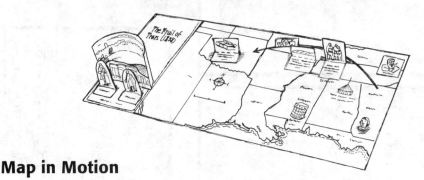

Map in Motion

Insert the Cherokee people piece in northern Georgia and move it to the Indian Territory (present-day Oklahoma) along what has come to be known as the Trail of Tears.

Map Points

In 1828, gold was discovered on Cherokee land in Georgia. White miners flocked there in search of riches. They harassed the Cherokees and were joined by other whites living nearby who felt they, not the Indians, should own the land. Instead of declaring war on the intruders, Cherokee elders went to court. They argued that their land grant treaty with the federal government ensured that they and their lands would be protected from harm by the state of Georgia.

By then, Cherokee leaders were well versed in United States government and law. After losing much land in the early 1800s due to wars with white settlers, the Cherokees centered their nation in northwestern Georgia, built farms, cotton plantations, and small towns. Cherokees also learned to read and write English to protect themselves from whites who tried to cheat them. A Cherokee named Sequoyah developed a Cherokee alphabet, which appeared in a newspaper called *The Cherokee Phoenix*, the first Native American newspaper in the United States. Using the U.S. government as a model, the Cherokees wrote laws and elected leaders.

But all these measures could not protect the Cherokees. In 1830, President Andrew Jackson signed the Indian Removal Act, which required Native American tribes east of the Mississippi River to exchange their lands for land west of the river. Many tribes were forced to move west, including the five major Indian nations in the Southeast: the Cherokees, Chickasaws, Choctaws, Seminoles, and Creeks. The Choctaws were moved out first, and then the Chickasaws. Seminoles led by the great warrior Chief Osceola and Creeks who resisted were driven out in chains. Many died of hunger or frost on the way west.

After suffering defeats in the Georgia courts, the Cherokees' case reached the U.S. Supreme Court in 1832. The court, led by Chief Justice John Marshall, ruled that the U.S. government must protect the Cherokees and their lands. However, since only the president could send in troops to assist the Indians, Jackson refused to help. He told John Marshall—his political enemy—to enforce the court decision himself. The betrayed Cherokees were split over what to do. Some moved west, while others wanted to keep fighting in courts. Still others were paid to sign a treaty giving up their lands. In May 1838, without warning, 7,000 federal troops started rounding up Cherokees in military camps and forts. Cherokee homes, even graves, were looted by neighboring whites.

Most of the nearly 16,000 captured Cherokees were forced to move west on the journey known as the Trail of Tears. They moved on foot, horseback, and in wagons. Their destination, about 1,200 miles away, was the Indian Territory (present-day Oklahoma). The march began in the hot summer, when there was little rain. Many Cherokees became sick from diseases that spread in the camps and forts; others became infected as they made their way through swamps and forests. Then winter brought snow, ice, and bitter cold. Between 2,000 and 4,000 tribe members died along the way. In Oklahoma, the survivors had to start over and rebuild their lives. Deaths continued as disease took its toll on those weakened by the long journey west.

Teaching With the Map

1. **What does the map show?** *(It shows the Trail of Tears, the route taken by Cherokees who were forced to leave their lands in Georgia and resettle in the Indian Territory.)*

2. **Why did the Cherokees go to court in the 1830s?** *(They wanted the U.S. government to stand behind its treaty with the Cherokees and protect them from harm.)*

3. **What was the Indian Removal Act?** *(The act allowed the United States president to force Native American tribes to exchange their land for land out west.)*

4. **How is the diorama related to the Cherokees?** *(John Marshall was Chief Justice of the Supreme Court, depicted on the diorama background. As president, Andrew Jackson lived and worked in the White House. The two men clashed when Jackson challenged Marshall to enforce the Supreme Court's ruling in favor of the Cherokees.)*

5. **Why has the route that the Cherokees took been called the Trail of Tears?** *(The name expresses the loss of land, homes, and livelihoods, and of the hardships and loss of life the Cherokees experienced on their long journey to the Indian Territory.)*

More Map Work

Separate the class into five groups. Assign one of the five Indian nations of the Southeast to each group: Choctaw, Chickasaw, Cherokee, Creek, and Seminole. Challenge each group to report on their nation during the 1820s and 1830s. Students should draw maps that show where the people of each nation lived, where they were forced to move, and how they got there. They can illustrate the maps with pictures of life such as houses, clothing, food, games and toys, and so on.

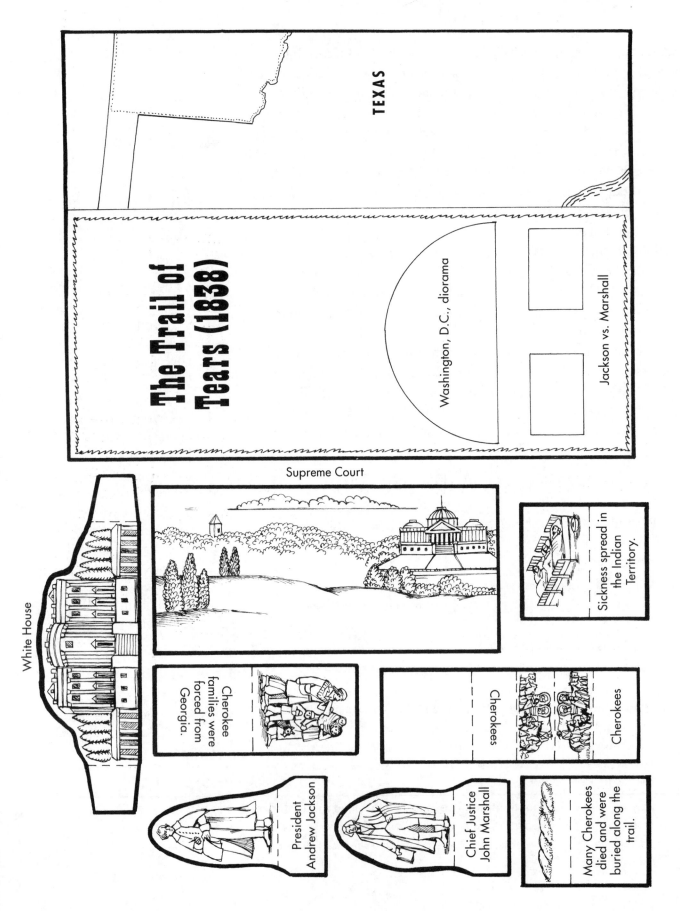

TEXAS

The Trail of
Tears (1838)

Washington, D.C., diorama

Jackson vs. Marshall

Supreme Court

White House

Sickness spread in
the Indian
Territory.

Cherokee
families were
forced from
Georgia.

Cherokees

Cherokees

President
Andrew Jackson

Chief Justice
John Marshall

Many Cherokees
died and were
buried along the
trail.

Interactive 3-D Maps: American History Scholastic Teaching Resources

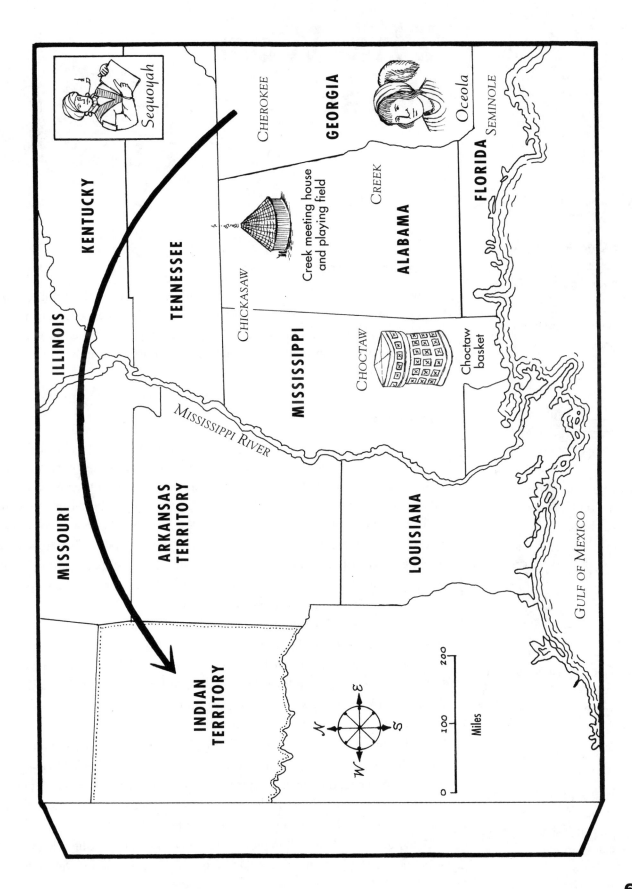

The Way West

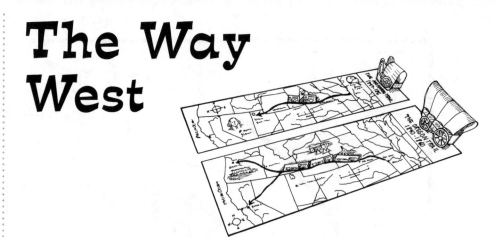

Maps in Motion

The two maps in this section show two different routes to the West. On the Oregon Trail map, insert three wagons at Independence, Missouri, and move them along the trail to Oregon City or California. On the Mormon Trail map, insert two Mormon handcarts at Nauvoo, Illinois, and move them along the trail to Salt Lake City.

Map Points

As the United States grew and prospered, the land beyond the Mississippi River became known as the West. In 1846, the Oregon Territory was added to the Union. Then in 1848, upper California became part of the nation as well. Soon pioneers were moving west to escape the crowded East and begin new lives.

The Oregon Trail stretched for 2,170 miles. Most families bound for Oregon joined wagon trains in Independence or St. Joseph, Missouri. They traveled in wagons fitted with a white canvas cover bowed over a wooden frame and pulled by oxen or mules. Because these covered wagons looked like sailing ships from a distance, pioneers called them *prairie schooners*.

Wagon trains began traveling at winter's end. In the spring and early summer, there was plenty of grass for animals to graze on. It took about two months for a wagon train to cross the Great Plains. At the Platte River Valley, in what is today Nebraska, wagons followed the river's south bank to Fort Kearney. Pioneers took the wheels off their wagons and turned the wagons into flat-bottomed boats to cross the Platte River.

By the time a wagon train reached Fort Laramie, families needed rest and supplies. The difficult passage through the Rocky Mountains lay ahead. During this steep part of the journey, many people tossed iron stoves and other heavy items from their wagons to lighten the load. At a 20-mile-wide stretch of grassy meadows called South Pass, the wagons crossed the mountains.

A few miles past Fort Hall in present-day Idaho the trail to California (and gold at Sutter's Fort) split off from the trail to Oregon. Those bound for Oregon followed

Mapmaking

1. Follow the instructions on page 5 for making both maps and moving pieces.

2. Cut out the Mormon handcart and bend, as shown.

3. Fold the end flaps along the dashed lines. Tape as shown.

4. Tape the handcart to the right of the Mormon Trail in the space provided.

5. Repeat steps 2 to 4 to make the prairie schooner.

6. Tape the prairie schooner to the right of the Oregon Trail map in the space provided.

the Snake River to the Blue Mountains. The journey of five months or more—full of hardships, hazards, and death—ended as families decided where to settle.

In 1846, the Mormons began a similar journey west. The Mormons were followers of Joseph Smith, who founded the Mormon Church in Fayette, New York, in 1830. Smith and his followers moved west to Illinois, where they built the village of Nauvoo in 1839. By 1844, about 20,000 Mormons had settled there, fueling anti-Mormon sentiment. When Smith was killed in 1844, Brigham Young became the leader of the Mormons.

Young led the Mormons west. They spent the harsh winter near the Missouri River (close to present-day Omaha) and then continued west in the spring of 1847. The first Mormons traveled in wagons. By the late 1850s, however, thousands of Mormons made the trek west pulling or pushing two-wheeled handcarts packed with food and other provisions. The Mormons followed the Oregon Trail but, fearful of attacks by unsympathetic pioneers, they took a route about a day's ride north of the trail. Along the way, Young left markers, such as buffalo skulls, on which he wrote messages for Mormons who would come later. This route became known as the Mormon Trail.

At Fort Bridger, the Mormons deviated from the Oregon Trail and turned their wagons southwest. Upon reaching the desert near the Great Salt Lake, Young declared that the Mormons had found their new home. That home became Salt Lake City, Utah.

Teaching With the Maps

1. **What do the maps show?** *(One map shows the Oregon Trail with the route to California that settlers and gold seekers took in the 1840s and 1850s. The other shows the trail the Mormons took to the Great Salt Lake.)*

2. **Why were covered wagons called prairie schooners?** *(Because of their canvas covers, the wagons looked like sailing ships from a distance.)*

3. **What natural features did wagon trains cross on their way to Oregon?** *(They crossed the Great Plains, rivers such as the Platte, and the Rocky Mountains.)*

4. **Why did pioneers throw away iron stoves and other items as they crossed the Rocky Mountains?** *(They wanted to lighten their wagonloads as they crossed the steep mountains.)*

5. **Why did the Mormons move west?** *(They were escaping religious persecution.)*

6. **Where and when did the Mormons' journey end?** *(It ended near the Great Salt Lake when Brigham Young declared they had found their new home.)*

More Map Work

Ask students to research the Oregon Trail and the Mormon Trail to locate landmarks such as Chimney Rock, Native American regions, and shortcuts on their maps. Then challenge them to do one of the activities below and mark the appropriate landmarks and routes on their maps.

- Investigate what happened at Donner Pass in 1846. What caused the tragedy?

- Search for information about the 1842 expedition led by John C. Frémont. Who really wrote the report about his expedition?

- Compare the Oregon Trail to the route that Lewis and Clark took. (See page 54.)

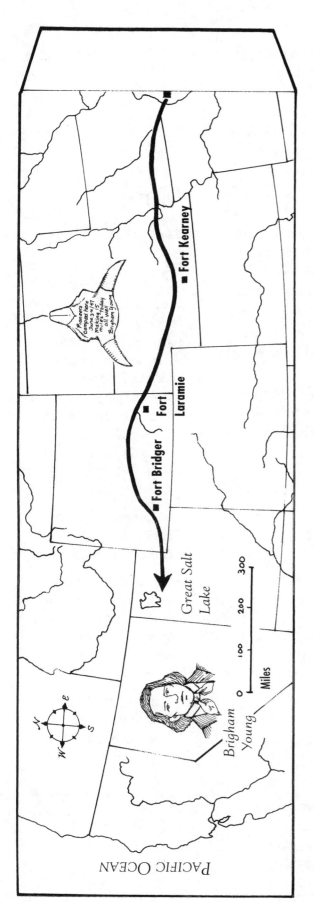

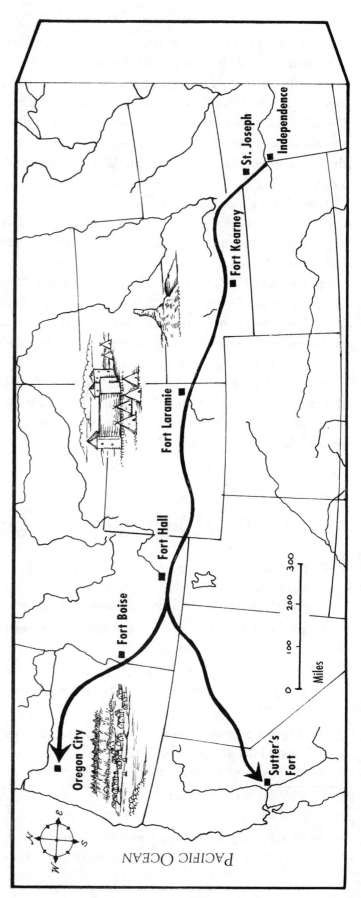

Interactive 3-D Maps: American History   Scholastic Teaching Resources

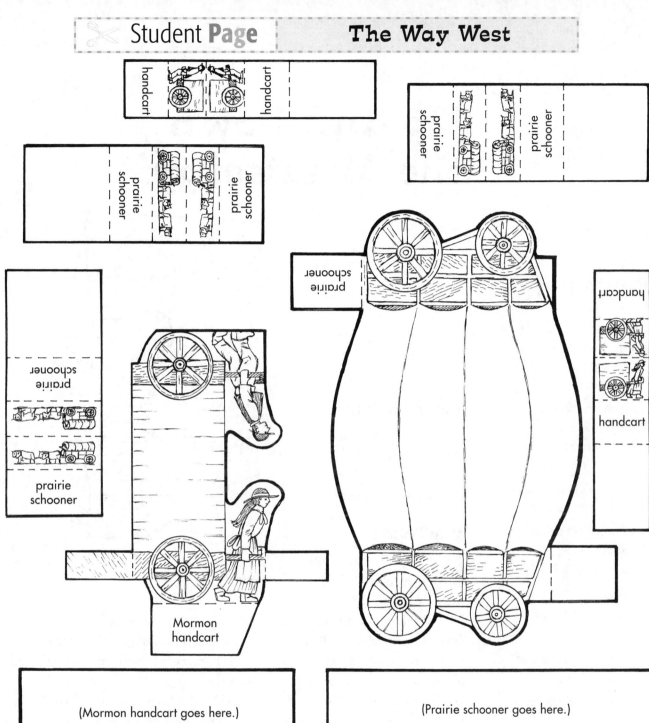

handcart

handcart

prairie schooner

prairie schooner

prairie schooner

prairie schooner

prairie schooner

prairie schooner

handcart

handcart

Mormon handcart

(Mormon handcart goes here.)

THE MORMON TRAIL 1847–1860

Joseph Smith

Nauvoo

(Prairie schooner goes here.)

THE OREGON TRAIL 1840–1860

Up and Down
the Mississippi

Mapmaking

1. Follow the instructions on page 5 for making the map, the moving piece, and the other pieces.

2. Guide students in writing the two-letter abbreviation for each state on the map.

3. Tape the other pieces on the map as follows:

   • the flatboat below Rock Island

   • the raft by the river in Wisconsin

   • the waterfall near Minneapolis

   • the sugarcane above New Orleans

   • the cotton bales below Memphis

Map in Motion

Insert and move a steam-powered riverboat up and down the Mississippi River.

Map Points

By the end of the 1840s and into the 1850s, the now transcontinental United States experienced major economic expansion and technological development. More and more, the nation's commercial growth relied on traffic on inland waterways. Fleets of steam-powered riverboats sailed up and down the Mississippi and other great rivers.

The Mississippi River flows about 2,350 miles from its source, Lake Itasca in Minnesota, to the Gulf of Mexico. Spanish explorer Hernando de Soto was probably the first European to discover the Mississippi River in 1541. French explorers Marquette and Joliet (see page 22) explored the lower Mississippi; then, in 1682, La Salle explored the lower Mississippi and claimed the river and its valley for France. With the Louisiana Purchase in 1803, the entire Mississippi River system became part of the United States. The Mississippi River linked the North and the South just as the Erie Canal, and later the railroads, linked the East and the West.

By 1840, the American South produced more cotton than any other place in the world. The cotton was shipped to textile mills in New England and across the Atlantic Ocean to England and other countries; about 75 percent of England's cotton came from the South. Steamboats (also known as

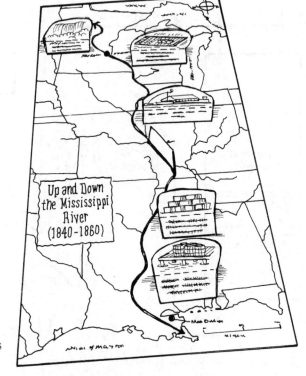

Up and Down
the Mississippi
River
(1840-1860)

riverboats, paddleboats, sternwheelers, and showboats) picked up and transported bales of cotton down the Mississippi River to New Orleans, which was the major exporting and importing center on the Gulf of Mexico. In New Orleans, the boats might load up with barrels of sugarcane syrup or imported manufactured goods such as cloth. They carried these goods and passengers north to cities and towns, such as St. Louis, where settlers joining wagon trains were in need of supplies.

River currents also carried flatboats loaded with freight from north to south. Lumber, too, made the journey down the Mississippi for delivery wherever homes and businesses were being built. Lumber was harvested from the vast forests in Illinois, Iowa, Wisconsin, and Minnesota. Logs were lashed together to form huge river rafts on which living and cooking houses were built for the raft rowers and other crew. A boat was also carried on the raft in case of emergency.

Samuel Clemens, the author of *Tom Sawyer* and *Huckleberry Finn*, was trained as a riverboat pilot on the Mississippi River. He took his pen name Mark Twain from a river navigation expression, "by the mark, twain"—a river call that meant the water was 12 feet or two fathoms deep, which was safe for sailing. Clemens witnessed and described how Mississippi River traffic helped transform the United States into an industrial power.

More Map Work

Challenge students to find out more about the Mississippi River by exploring one of the following topics:

- its tributaries, including the Missouri River, the Ohio River, the Arkansas River, and so on

- the importance of the Mississippi Delta

- the river's connection to the Great Lakes– St. Lawrence Seaway

- the areas along the river where Native American tribes made their homes

- Mark Twain's stories about life on the river

Ask students to include maps, or add details to the map for this lesson, in their presentations.

Teaching With the Map

1. **What does the map show?** *(It shows the route traveled by boats and rafts up and down the Mississippi River.)*

2. **How did the United States gain possession of the river?** *(The river was part of the Louisiana Purchase from France in 1803.)*

3. **What parts of the United States did the Mississippi River link?** *(It linked the North with the South.)*

4. **What kinds of traffic moved along the river?** *(There were steamboats, flatboats, and rafts.)*

5. **What did the traffic transport up and down the river?** *(Passengers, cotton bales, barrels of sugarcane syrup, manufactured goods such as cloth, and raw materials such as lumber.)*

6. **Who was Mark Twain? What connection does his name have with rivers?** *(He was the famous American author Samuel Clemens, who once worked as a riverboat pilot on the Mississippi. If a person called "by the mark, twain," that meant the river was at least 12 feet deep, which was safe for sailing.)*

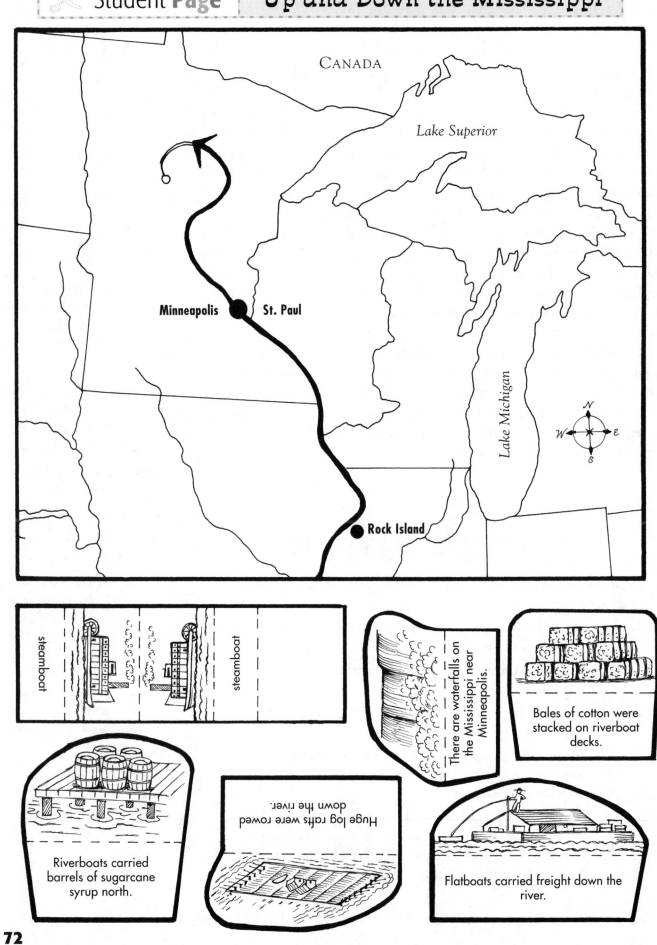

CANADA

Lake Superior

Minneapolis ● St. Paul

Lake Michigan

● Rock Island

N
W · E
S

steamboat

steamboat

There are waterfalls on the Mississippi near Minneapolis.

Bales of cotton were stacked on riverboat decks.

Riverboats carried barrels of sugarcane syrup north.

Huge log rafts were rowed down the river.

Flatboats carried freight down the river.

Interactive 3-D Maps: American History Scholastic Teaching Resources

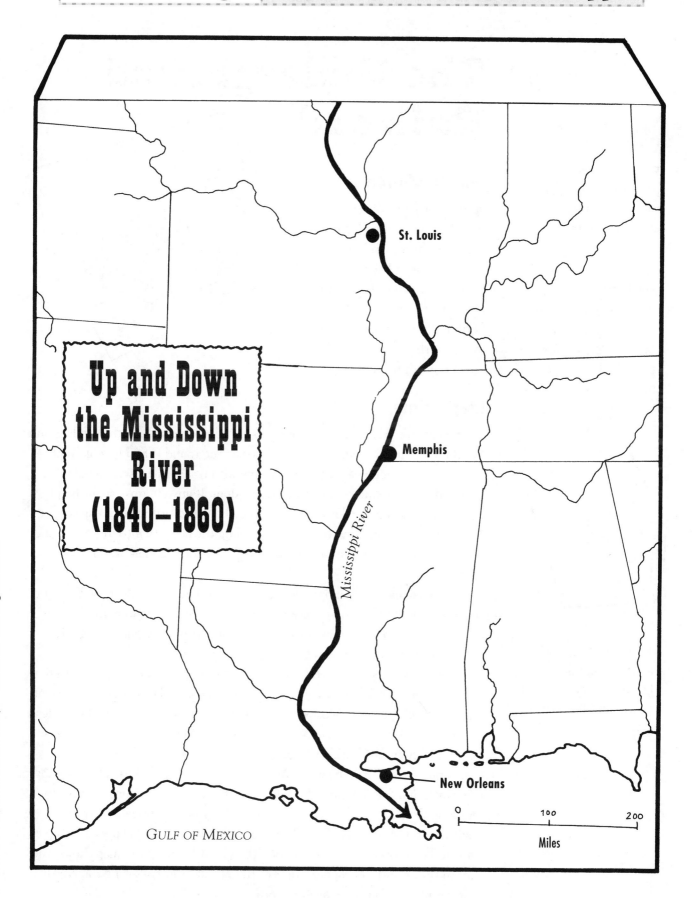

Up and Down
the Mississippi
River
(1840–1860)

St. Louis

Memphis

Mississippi River

New Orleans

GULF OF MEXICO

0   100   200

Miles

Mapmaking

1. Follow the instructions on page 5 for making the map, the moving pieces, and other pieces.

2. At the top of the map, fold up the top and side flaps.

3. Cut out the North Star "drinking gourd" piece. Tape it to the top flap and side flaps of the map, as shown.

4. Tape Harriet Tubman above Philadelphia and Levi and Catherine Coffin above the Ohio River in Indiana.

The Underground Railroad

Map in Motion

Insert the group on foot at Cairo, Illinois, moving it north to Chicago and then across the Great Lakes to Detroit. Insert the group with the horse at Washington, D.C., moving it north to Philadelphia and Canada. Then, insert the ship at Portsmouth, Virginia, and move it north to Boston.

Map Points

From about 1830 to 1860, Americans heard whispers about the Underground Railroad. It was neither a railroad nor underground. The Underground Railroad was a group of courageous people who risked their lives to help enslaved African Americans escape to freedom. If anyone was caught helping escapees, he or she faced prison or death by hanging. With the passage of the Missouri Compromise in 1820, a line dividing the country into free states and slave-holding states was established. Slavery was forbidden above latitude 36°30'.

A code enabled the Underground Railroad to function in secrecy. Escaping slaves were referred to as *passengers*. A house in which they were hidden was called a *station* and the house owner was a *stationmaster*. A *conductor* guided people on their long journeys to freedom in the North.

Some conductors pretended to be slave traders to gain access to people working on plantations. Slaves who they helped escape usually hid by day and traveled at night to avoid detection. Most walked. Some rode stolen horses. All of them feared for their lives as they tried to avoid armed patrols and navigated through rivers, forests, and swamps—usually without having eaten for days.

Conductors and passengers on the Underground Railroad used the position of the North Star for direction. They learned the words to the song "Follow the Drinking Gourd," which itself was a code telling how to travel north from Alabama and Mississippi. The "drinking gourd" was the Big Dipper, a group of stars in the constellation Ursa Major—the Great Bear. As the map shows, the stars in the "gourd," or dipper, point to the North Star. Following the North Star meant a person was traveling north.

Once passengers on the Underground Railroad reached the first station, such as the one in Cairo, Illinois, they were fed, clothed, and hidden in secret rooms or tunnels by the stationmaster. Then, they were directed to the next station by a conductor, and so on. Quakers Levi and Catherine Coffin assisted about 3,000 escaping slaves at their station in southern Indiana. But even when people reached stations they were far from being safe. Slave owners hired slave catchers to retrieve what they considered to be their property. By law, owners could forcibly take back their slaves—no matter where they were found in the United States.

Only in Canada were escaping slaves truly free and safe because Canadian law prohibited slavery and slave catchers. People who reached Chicago took boats across the Great Lakes to Detroit and then went to Canada. Some who made it to Portsmouth, Virginia, were sent by abolitionist southerners by ship to Boston, where they could stay or continue by land to Canada. Those who made it to New York City either remained there or continued north.

Many former slaves became conductors on the Underground Railroad themselves. In 1849, Harriet Tubman escaped to Philadelphia from Maryland. A few months later, she returned for her sister and her sister's children. Harriet Tubman returned to the South 18 more times and took about 300 African Americans north, including her parents. As she said, she never lost a single passenger.

Teaching With the Map

1. **What does the map show?** (It shows routes of the Underground Railroad, which helped transport escaping African Americans from the South to the northern United States and Canada.)

2. **What was the Underground Railroad?** (It was a system of escape routes and people who aided those escaping from slavery.)

3. **What code words were used by people on the Underground Railroad and why?** (Code words such as passenger, conductor, station, and stationmaster were used for secrecy to protect people associated with the Underground Railroad. If caught, they could be imprisoned or put to death.)

4. **How did passengers on the Underground Railroad find their way?** (After reaching the first station, slaves were directed to each succeeding station. People in Alabama and Mississippi learned the words to "Follow the Drinking Gourd," located the North Star, and used it to navigate.)

5. **Why was Canada the final destination for many African Americans?** (In the United States, an enslaved person could be recaptured and forced to return to slavery. Canada had outlawed slavery and slave catchers.)

6. **Who was Harriet Tubman?** (She was a former passenger on the Underground Railroad who returned to the South many times to take other slaves out of bondage.)

More Map Work

Dozens of heavily traveled Underground Railroad routes extended from the Kansas Territory and Iowa to the New England states. Routes and connections also led south into Mexico and into the western United States. For excellent resources on this and other topics, visit the National Park Service National Underground Railroad Network to Freedom Web site at http://209.10.16.21/TEMPLATE/FrontEnd/learn_b4.cfm. Challenge students to research these routes and add them to their maps. Also have students delve more deeply into the life of Harriet Tubman and chronicle her movements on the Underground Railroad by drawing a story map.

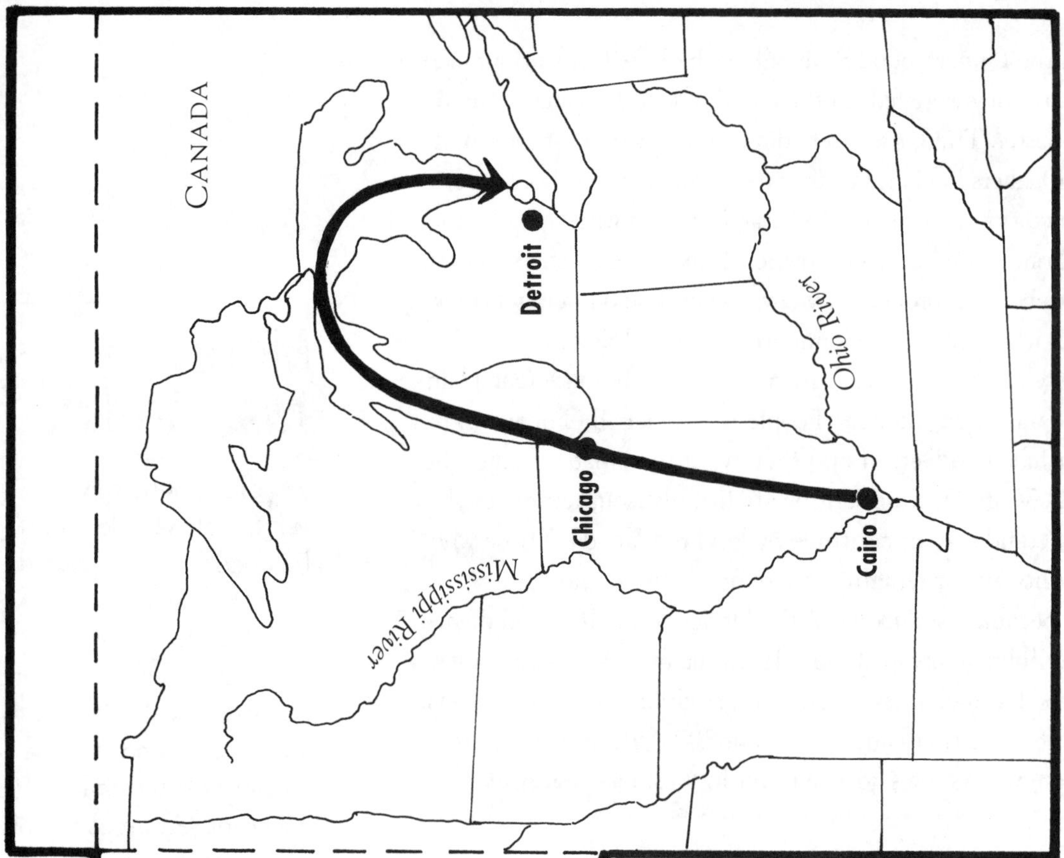

CANADA

Detroit

Ohio River

Chicago

Mississippi River

Cairo

escaping by ship

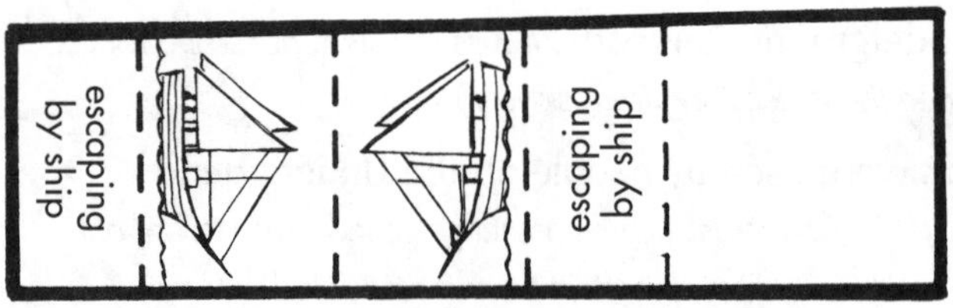

escaping by ship

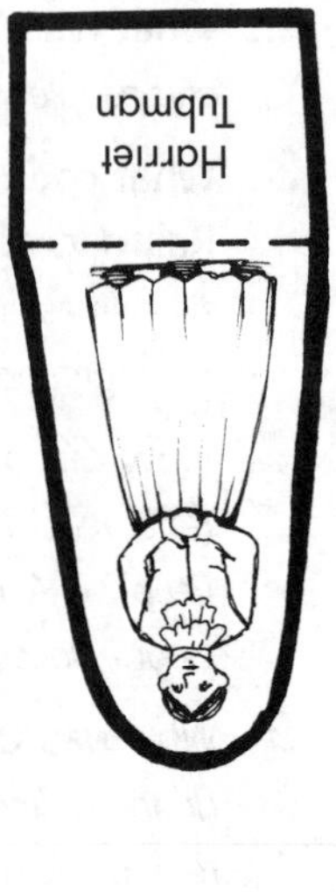

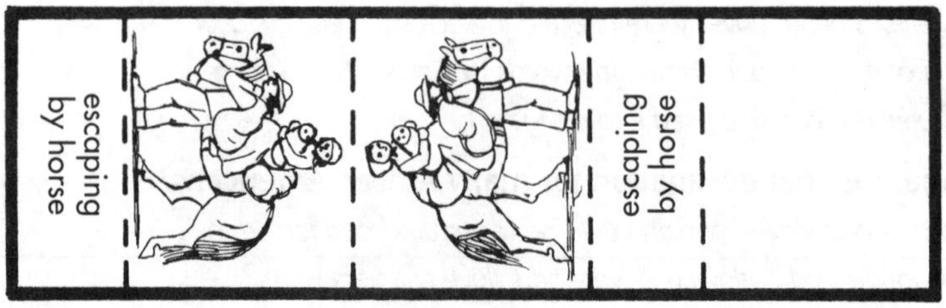

escaping by horse

escaping by horse

Harriet Tubman

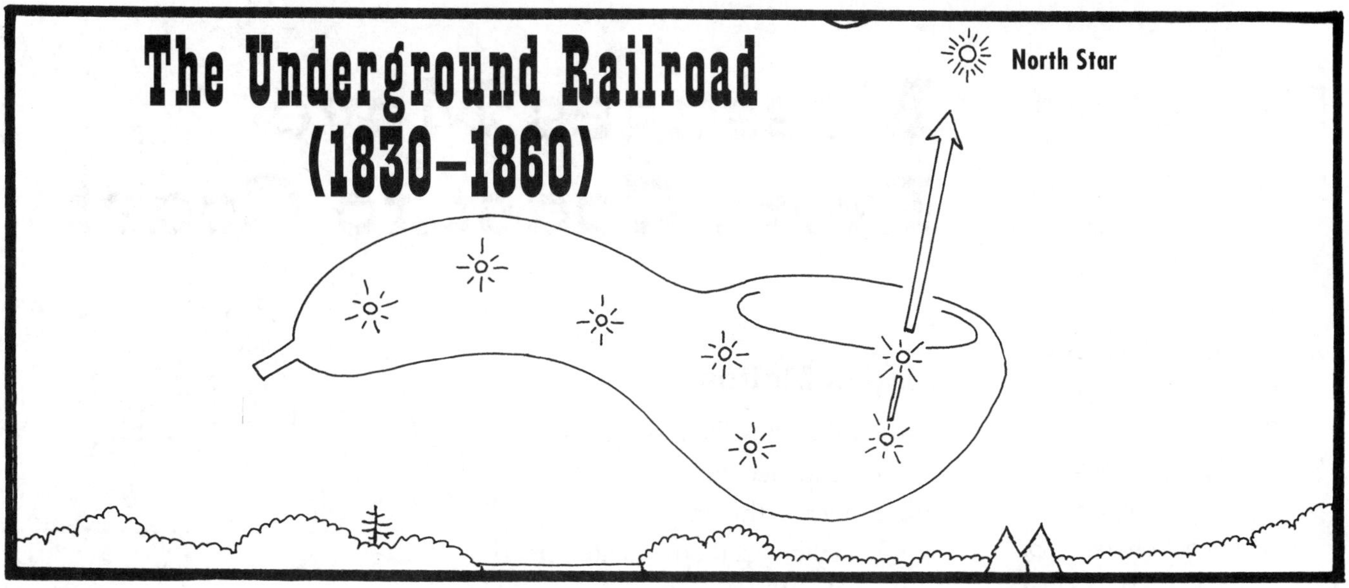

The Underground Railroad (1830–1860)

North Star

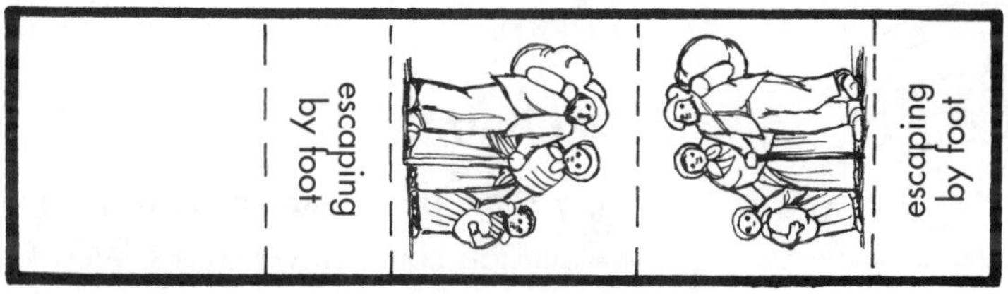

escaping by boat

escaping by foot

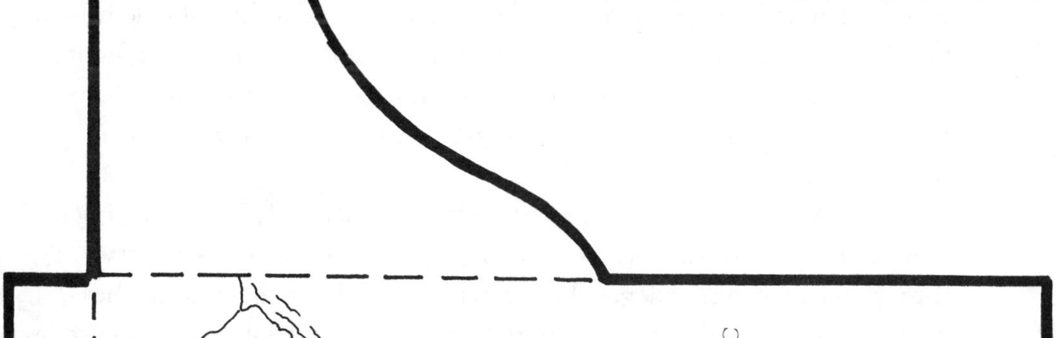

ATLANTIC OCEAN

Boston

Montreal

New York City

Philadelphia

Portsmouth

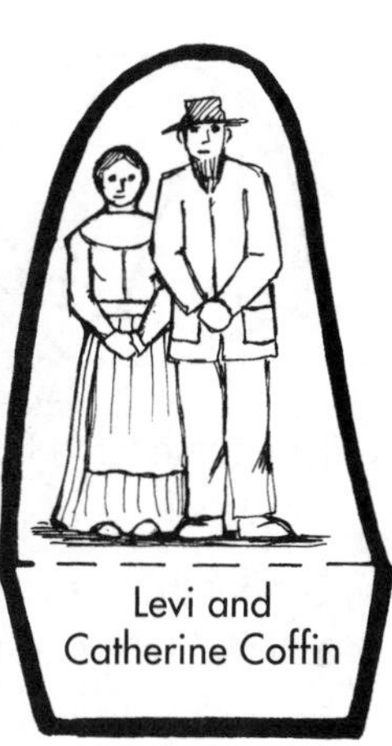

Levi and Catherine Coffin

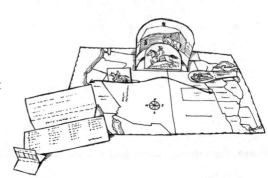

Mapmaking

1. Follow the instructions on page 5 for making the map and the moving pieces.

2. Cut out the Pony Express rider and the station pieces.

3. Fold back the TAPE tabs on the station piece. Tape them on the map so the piece curves, as shown.

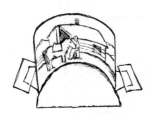

4. Fold back the upper and lower portions of the rider piece along the dashed lines. Tape the upper portion to the lower portion as shown.

5. Tape the rider in front of the station.

6. Cut out the telegraph key and fold so the text can be read.

7. Tape the telegraph key above Independence, Missouri.

Messages Move From Coast to Coast

Map in Motion

Insert the Pony Express rider at Independence, Missouri, and move it across the frontier to San Francisco, California. Later, remove the Pony Express piece and insert the telegraph wires, moving it from Independence to San Francisco.

Map Points

By 1860, there were many ways in which mail, newspapers, and other information could travel to the West Coast. Wagons picked up mail in Missouri; in about four months, it was delivered to California. Steamships also delivered mail between New York City and San Francisco, California. That trip, around the southern tip of South America, took about a month. In 1858, the Butterfield Overland Mail Company dispatched stagecoaches, which cut delivery time to around 25 days.

Samuel Morse applied for a patent for the *telegraph* in 1837. By tapping on a switch key, Morse was able to send long and short pulses of electricity through a wire to a sounder at the receiving end. The sounder made clicks, which a person could translate into the letters of the alphabet using the code Morse invented: a long click translated into a dash and a short click into a dot. Telegraph messages could be sent long distances, received, and translated within minutes. By 1860, thousands of miles of telegraph wires stretched from East Coast cities all the way to St. Joseph, Missouri. However, there was still no way for urgent news to reach the West Coast. To remedy that situation, William H. Russell started the Pony Express.

Russell was convinced that young men riding day and night could make the journey between St. Joseph and Sacramento, California, in 10 days, provided they could frequently change horses and riders. Russell had 190 stations built along a 1,966-mile route he mapped out. One hundred and sixty-five *relay stations* were built 10 to 20 miles apart (depending on the terrain) to provide riders with fresh horses. Twenty-five home or *swing stations* were built 50 to 100 miles apart in which riders ate and slept after they were relieved by other riders. As soon as a station keeper heard hoof beats, he saddled a fresh horse so the exchange could take place within two minutes.

One Pony Express advertisement read as follows: "Wanted, young skinny, wiry fellows not over eighteen, must be expert riders willing to risk death daily, orphans preferred. Wages $25 a week. Apply Central Overland Express." In addition to wages, riders received bed and board. On April 3, 1860, one rider left St. Joseph and headed west to Sacramento, California. Another rider headed east from Sacramento to St. Joseph. In their pouches, they carried mail, newspapers, legal documents, and urgent messages such as those sent by telegraph to St. Joseph. Ten days later, each rider delivered his pouch as promised by the Pony Express.

Until November 1861, Pony Express riders and station keepers overcame floods, blizzards, desert heat, harsh terrain, and attacks by bandits and hostile tribes. The Pony Express brought news of Lincoln's inauguration and the firing on Fort Sumter to the West Coast. Only one pouch was lost. Yet, in spite of its efficiency and the heroism of its riders, the Pony Express never made a profit nor received a government contract to deliver mail. Telegraph poles were being constructed along the same route used by the Pony Express. In October 1861, the first transcontinental telegraph message was received in California. Within a month, the Pony Express went out of business.

More Map Work

Challenge students to do one of the following projects:

- Compare and contrast their Pony Express maps to the maps of the Oregon and Mormon Trails.

- With the help of a topographical map of the United States, indicate on their Pony Express maps where a rider encountered plains, mountains, deserts, and so on.

Teaching With the Map

1. **What does the map show?** *(It shows the route taken by Pony Express riders to and from St. Joseph, Missouri. It also shows the path of the first transcontinental telegraph wires.)*

2. **Why was there a need for the Pony Express?** *(People living in the West wanted to receive mail, newspapers, and urgent messages more quickly.)*

3. **How did the Pony Express work?** *(A rider carrying mail rode to relay stations where he changed horses. Then, he stopped at a home station, and another rider took over.)*

4. **Why did the Pony Express go out of business?** *(It never made a profit nor received a government contract to deliver mail. When the transcontinental telegraph was completed, there was no need for the Pony Express.)*

5. **Who invented the telegraph, and how did it work?** *(Samuel Morse invented the telegraph and the Morse code. By pressing a key, long and short electrical pulses were sent along a wire to a sounder at the receiving end. Clicks from the sounder were translated into the dots and dashes of the Morse code.)*

6. **Look at the first transcontinental message. Use the Morse code to decipher the message.** *("May the Union be perpetual.")*

7. **Why was this message so timely?** *(The message was timely because the Civil War was being fought at that time.)*

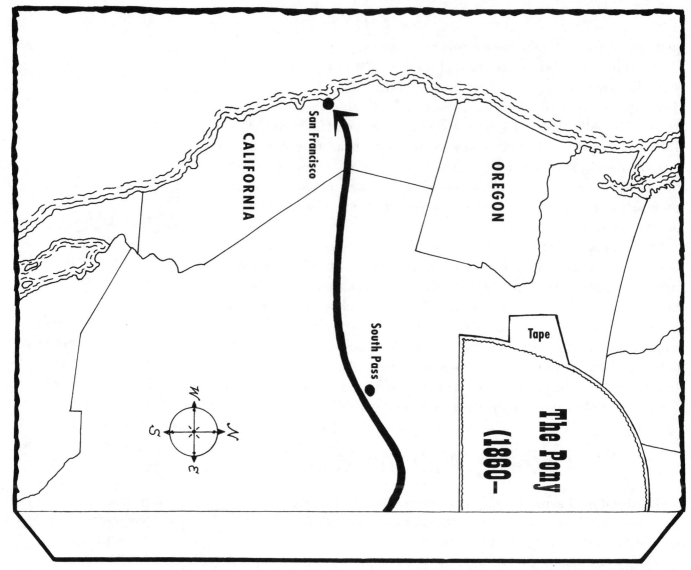

CALIFORNIA

OREGON

San Francisco

South Pass

Tape

The Pony (1860–

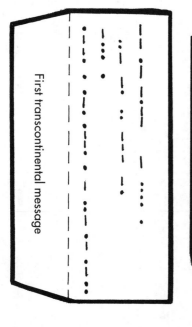

First transcontinental message

Tape

Tape

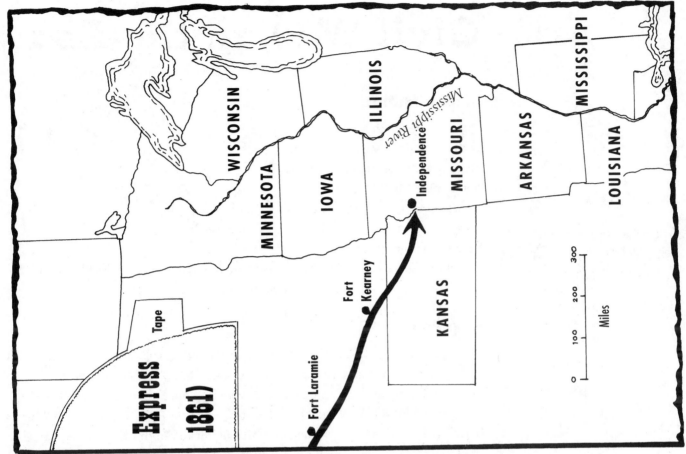

Express (1861)

Tape

WISCONSIN

ILLINOIS

MISSISSIPPI

MINNESOTA

IOWA

Mississippi River

Independence

MISSOURI

ARKANSAS

LOUISIANA

Fort Kearney

KANSAS

Fort Laramie

0 100 200 300

Miles

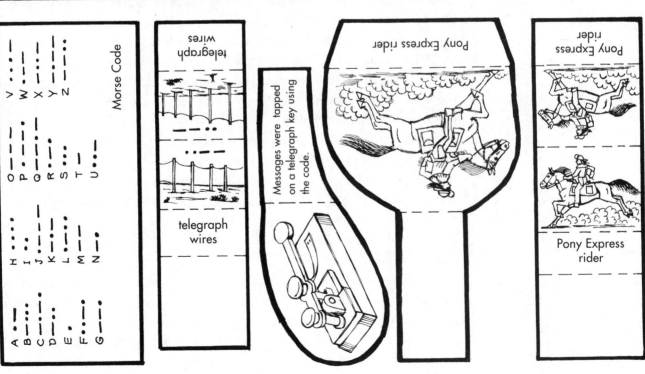

Morse Code

A ·—
B —···
C —·—·
D —··
E ·
F ··—·
G ——·

H ····
I ··
J ·———
K —·—
L ·—··
M ——
N —·

O ———
P ·——·
Q ——·—
R ·—·
S ···
T —
U ··—

V ···—
W ·——
X —··—
Y —·——
Z ——··

telegraph wires

Messages were tapped on a telegraph key using the code.

Pony Express rider

Pony Express rider

Pony Express rider

Civil War on the Sea

Map in Motion

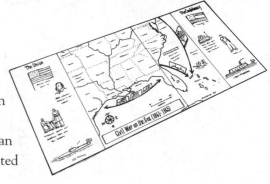

Insert three Union ships in the Gulf of Mexico and move them to blockade southern ports. Insert the U.S.S. *Constitution* in the Atlantic Ocean off the southeast coast of the United States and move it toward the Caribbean Sea. Then insert the Confederate blockade runner *Robert E. Lee* off the Georgia coast and move it toward the Bahamas.

Mapmaking

Follow the instructions on page 5 for making the map and the moving pieces.

Map Points

By February 1861, seven southern states (South Carolina, Mississippi, Florida, Alabama, Georgia, Louisiana, and Texas) had seceded from the Union and formed the Confederacy. In March, Abraham Lincoln was inaugurated President of the United States. Then on April 12, the Civil War began with a Confederate attack on Fort Sumter in South Carolina. Although the Confederacy had no navy at the time, it was certain that England and France would come to its aid because both countries were dependent economically on southern cotton and other trade items. President Lincoln and General-in-Chief Winfield Scott also recognized the importance of cotton to the southern economy. They decided to blockade southern ports to prevent both the exportation of cotton and the importation of manufactured goods, especially war supplies.

The Union sent 41 ships to patrol waters off the coast of the Confederate States. By 1862, that number had risen to 427 ships, which included newly built ships as well as sailboats, tugboats, and other vessels that the Union Navy turned into gunships. The ships formed a blockade that patrolled the waters from Richmond, Virginia, down the Atlantic coast, around the tip of Florida, and back up the west coast of Florida to the southern ports in the Gulf of Mexico.

The Union blockade was difficult to enforce because the southern coastline extended over 3,500 miles. When the Confederates realized that no naval help from European allies was coming, they built their own navy, including ships such as the *Robert E. Lee* and *Stonewall Jackson*, which served as *blockade runners*. Blockade runners attempted to slip past the Union patrol ships so they could carry cotton to Bermuda or Nassau and return with vital manufactured goods. From 1861 to 1865, Union ships such as the U.S.S. *Constitution* captured or destroyed more than 1,500 blockade runners, but hundreds of other ships slipped through. Ultimately, the blockade was a success because it forced up prices in the South and resulted in a shortage of many goods.

Civil War battles fought on the sea changed naval history. When the wooden Union ship, the *Merrimack*, was sunk off the coast of Virginia, the Confederates raised it, renamed it the *Virginia*, and bolted iron plates onto it. The *Merrimack-Virginia* became the first *ironclad ship*, which could withstand cannon fire and being burned; it also could ram a wooden warship to splinters. In response to this new weapon, Union naval engineer John Ericsson designed the *Monitor*—an ironclad with revolving gun turrets. On March 9, 1862, the two ironclad ships battled off the coast of Virginia. After more than four hours, the *Merrimack-Virginia* withdrew from the battle, but neither side won. Two months later, when the Confederates had to flee Norfolk, they blew up their ironclad ship. The Union, however, built more ironclads. The day of the wooden warship was over.

Another famous naval battle involved the *H. L. Hunley*, a Confederate submarine with a *pole* (spar) sticking out of its bow. At the end of the pole was a *mine* (called a *torpedo*). As one man steered the submarine, seven others cranked the propeller to make it move. On February 17, 1864, the *Hunley* made its way into Charleston Harbor and disappeared about six feet below the surface. About four miles out to sea, it rammed the Union warship *Housatonic*. The mine exploded, and the *Hunley* became the first submarine ever to sink a warship. However, the *Hunley* mysteriously sank that night. In 1995, the wreck of the *Hunley* was found outside of Charleston Harbor, and it was raised in August 2000. No one knows yet why the submarine sank.

More Map Work

Challenge students to report on what happened during the battle between the *Monitor* and the *Merrimack* in the form of a time line, newspaper article, play, short story, series of drawings with captions, poem, or radio or television report.

Teaching With the Map

1. **What does the map show?** *(It shows part of the Union blockade of southern ports and a Confederate blockade runner trying to slip past the U.S.S.* Constitution.*)*

2. **What was the purpose of the blockade by the Union ships?** *(Its purpose was to prevent the Confederacy's exportation of cotton and importation of manufactured goods.)*

3. **What were blockade runners?** *(Blockade runners were Confederate ships that tried to slip past Union blockade vessels to reach Bermuda or Nassau.)*

4. **What were the *Monitor* and the *Merrimack*?** *(They were the first two ironclad ships, signaling the end of wooden warships. They fought each other.)*

5. **How did the *Hunley* change naval history?** *(It became the first submarine to sink an enemy warship.)*

The Union

United States naval flag

John Ericsson, designer of the Monitor

President Lincoln and General Scott plan the blockade.

U.S.S. Monitor

Civil War on the Sea (1861–1865)

NEBRASKA

KANSAS

(OKLAHOMA) INDIAN TERRITORY

IOWA

MISSOURI

ILLINOIS

INDIANA

OHIO

ARKANSAS

KENTUCKY

TENNESSEE

TEXAS

LOUISIANA

New Orleans

MISSISSIPPI

ALABAMA

GEORGIA

Galveston

Mobile

Savannah

GULF OF MEXICO

Miles

0   100   200

Interactive 3-D Maps: American History   Scholastic Teaching Resources

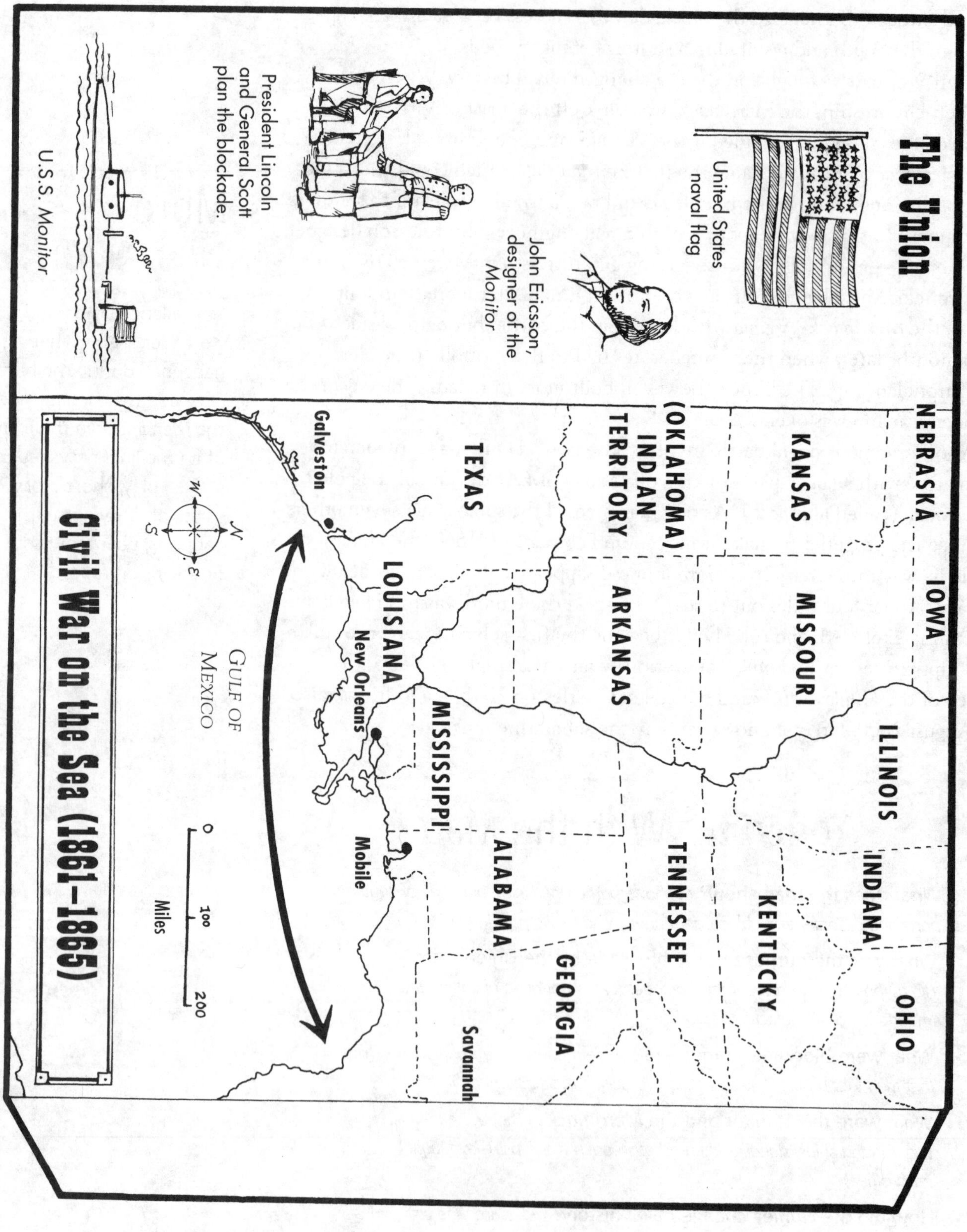

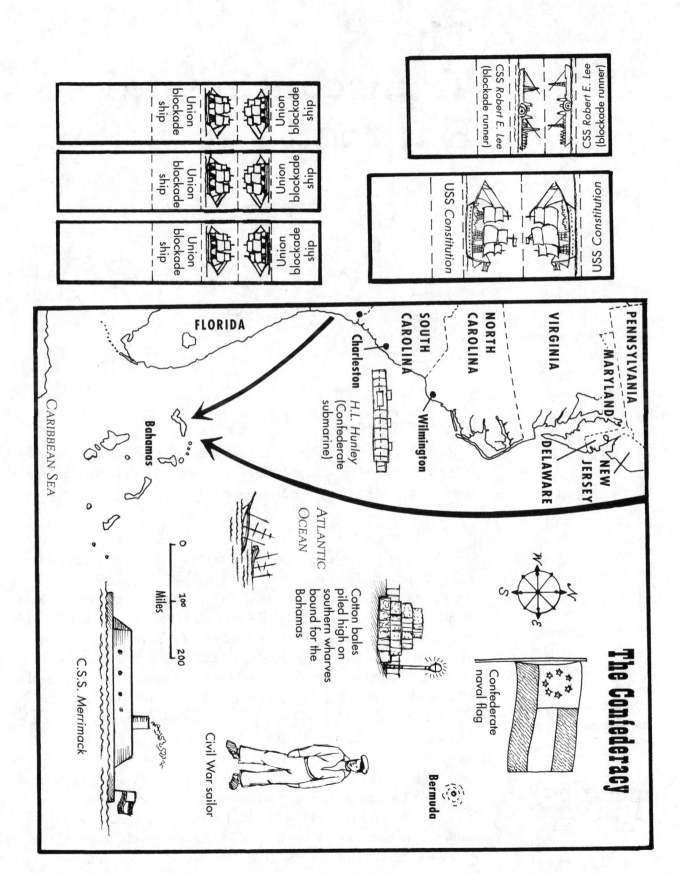

Union blockade ship

Union blockade ship

Union blockade ship

Union blockade ship

Union blockade ship

Union blockade ship

CSS *Robert E. Lee* (blockade runner)

CSS *Robert E. Lee* (blockade runner)

USS *Constitution*

USS *Constitution*

FLORIDA

SOUTH CAROLINA

NORTH CAROLINA

VIRGINIA

PENNSYLVANIA

MARYLAND

NEW JERSEY

DELAWARE

Charleston

Wilmington

H.L. Hunley (Confederate submarine)

CARIBBEAN SEA

Bahamas

ATLANTIC OCEAN

Cotton bales piled high on southern wharves bound for the Bahamas

0   100   200
Miles

C.S.S. Merrimack

Civil War sailor

Confederate naval flag

Bermuda

The Confederacy

Interactive 3-D Maps: American History   Scholastic Teaching Resources

Mapmaking

1. Follow the instructions on page 5 for making the map, the moving pieces, and other pieces.

2. Cut out the tunnel piece and fold the flaps under. Tape each flap over the word TAPE on the map so the tunnel curves.

3. Tape the eastern railroad network in the space above and between Omaha and Chicago.

4. Tape the golden spike above Promontory, Utah.

5. Cut out the remaining pieces. Tape the sides of the trestle bridge to the cliffs.

6. Slip the work train piece behind the bridge until it appears on the upper part of the bridge, as shown. Fold up the end tab at the bottom of the bridge. Move the end from the left side of the bridge to the right, making the train move. Tape the piece to the map.

The Transcontinental Railroad

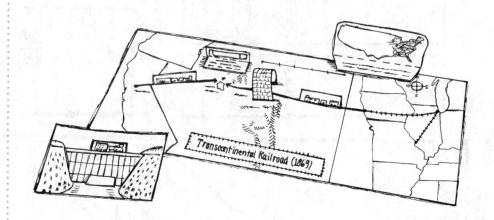

Transcontinental Railroad (1869)

Map in Motion

Insert the Union Pacific Railroad at Omaha and the Central Pacific Railroad at Sacramento. Move both trains until they meet at Promontory, Utah. Students can also move a workers' train across a trestle bridge.

Map Points

While pioneers moved west in wagon trains or on horseback, merchants and politicians in the East began to toss around the idea of a railroad line that would span the nation from ocean to ocean. In 1853, Congress sent survey teams to determine the most practical route for a railroad west of the Mississippi River; a network of railroads already existed east of the river. Compared with other forms of transportation, railroad travel was faster and more reliable, benefiting both individual passengers and business shipments. By extending this rail network to California, Congress envisioned economic, social, and political rewards that would result from speeding up the settlement of the West and from shipping raw materials and manufactured goods across the entire country.

In 1862, two railroad companies received land and money from Congress to construct bridges and tunnels and to lay tracks for a transcontinental railroad. The Union Pacific was given the task of building west from Omaha, Nebraska, while the Central Pacific would build east from Sacramento, California. In January 1863, the Central Pacific began work, but the Union Pacific was delayed until 1865 because of the Civil War. Both companies relied heavily on immigrant labor. The Central Pacific hired thousands of Chinese immigrants; many Irish immigrants joined Civil War veterans on the Union Pacific payroll. The hours were long, the pay was low, and the working conditions were dangerous and difficult. Workers blasted tunnels through mountains and then cleared the debris with pickaxes. To cross a river, they would construct a temporary, rickety trestle bridge over the river, lay tracks on the other side, and then ride across on a work train. This train had a bunk car in which the workmen slept. Once across the bridge, some workers stayed behind to build a stronger bridge that could hold the weight of a full train. The other workers moved forward, laying more tracks.

In 1869, workers from each railroad company approached Promontory, Utah, north of the Great Salt Lake. The Central Pacific had laid 690 miles of track from Sacramento, while the Union Pacific covered 1,086 miles from Omaha. In a ceremony on May 10, 1869, a golden spike was driven into the spot where the tracks met. Then, the locomotive on Union Pacific 119 and on Central Pacific's Jupiter inched toward each other and touched cowcatchers at the end of each locomotive. Within minutes, the entire nation received word by telegraph that the transcontinental railroad was complete. It was now possible to travel from the East Coast to the West Coast in less than 10 days.

More Map Work

By 1890, the United States had more than 200,000 miles of railroad tracks. Challenge groups of students to research on the Internet and draw maps of routes taken by the following railroad companies:

- Texas and Pacific
- Southern
- Atchison, Topeka & Santa Fe
- Northern Pacific
- Great Northern
- Illinois Central
- Pennsylvania
- Baltimore and Ohio
- New York Central

Teaching With the Map

1. **What does the map show?** *(It shows where tracks were laid to create the transcontinental railroad.)*

2. **Where did work begin and end?** *(Workers hired by the Central Pacific laid tracks from Sacramento, California, to Promontory, Utah. Union Pacific workers laid tracks from Omaha, Nebraska, to Promontory.)*

3. **Why did Congress support the building of a transcontinental railroad?** *(Congress envisioned the benefits of passenger and freight traveling by rail from coast to coast.)*

4. **Where did railroad workers come from?** *(Many were immigrants from China and Ireland. Others were Civil War veterans.)*

5. **Describe the working conditions.** *(The men worked long hours for low pay. The work was dangerous; for instance, blasting tunnels and building bridges.)*

6. **What happened at Promontory, Utah, on May 10, 1869?** *(The railroad was completed. A golden spike was driven into the tracks, the locomotives of the Central Pacific and Union Pacific touched, and word was sent across the country by telegraph of the momentous event.)*

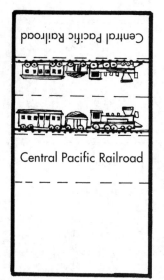

Central Pacific Railroad

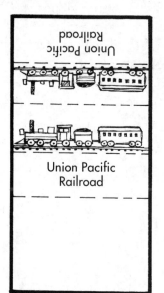

Union Pacific
Railroad

Work train
with bunk
car for
workers

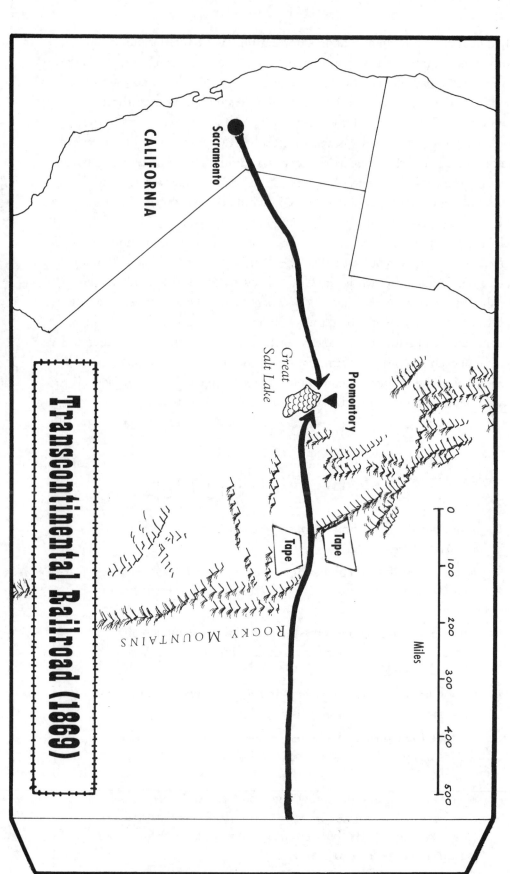

Transcontinental Railroad (1869)

CALIFORNIA

Sacramento

Great
Salt Lake

Promontory

Tape

Tape

ROCKY MOUNTAINS

Miles

0
100
200
300
400
500

Interactive 3-D Maps: American History Scholastic Teaching Resources

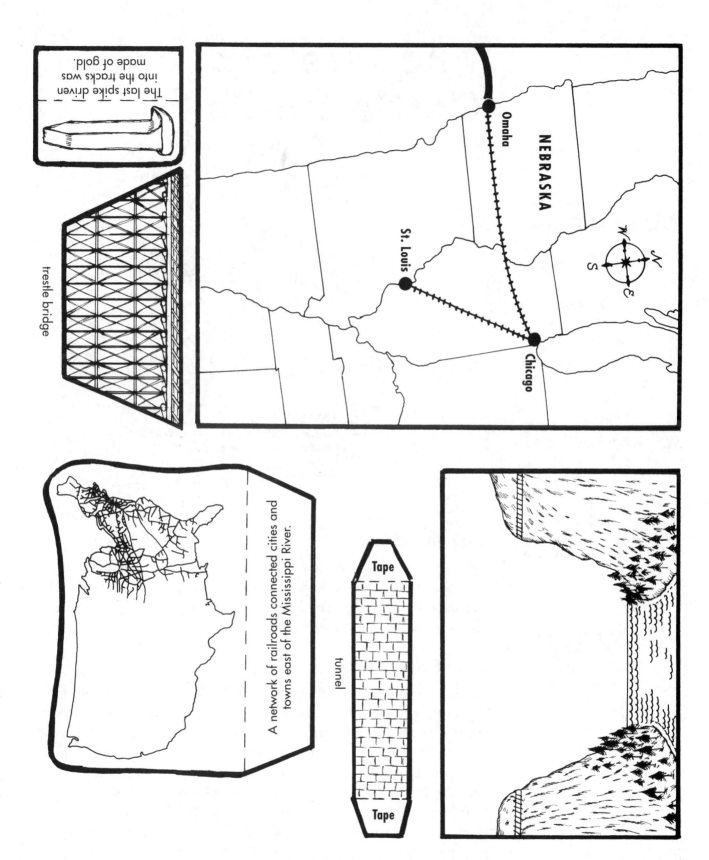

The last spike driven
into the tracks was
made of gold.

trestle bridge

Omaha

NEBRASKA

St. Louis

Chicago

N W S E

A network of railroads connected cities and
towns east of the Mississippi River.

Tape

tunnel

Tape

The Western Cattle Trails

The Western Cattle Trails (1866–1890)

Mapmaking

1. Follow the instructions on page 5 for making the map, the moving piece, and other pieces.

2. Tape the cowboy and chuck wagon next to the selected trail. Tape the longhorn steer at the start of the trail in Texas.

3. Below the map, cut open the buildings and railroad along the solid black lines. Fold the cut-out sections along the dashed lines to make them pop up, as shown.

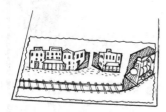

Map in Motion

Cut open one of the cattle trails: Goodnight-Loving, Western, Chisholm, or Shawnee. Then select a town on that trail and identify which railroad lines run through it. Insert the cattle piece at the beginning of the selected trail in Texas and move it to the town or railway.

Map Points

From the end of the Civil War until the 1890s, cowboys drove millions of cattle north from Texas to cow towns where the cattle was herded aboard railroad cars. The cattle was then shipped to slaughterhouses in Chicago and points east to meet the growing American demand for beef. Cattle barons, such as Charles Goodnight, owned huge ranches. Like others who controlled the cattle trade, Goodnight discovered that a steer worth only a few dollars in Texas was valued at $40 or more up north. All the ranchers had to do was deliver the cattle to railcars hundreds of miles away. That meant rounding up herds of cattle, branding every cow with an identifying mark (to prevent theft), and driving them slowly along the trail so the animals could fatten up on grass as they traveled. To brand cattle, two cowboys held down a cow while a third branded its side with letters, numbers, pictures, or geometric symbols using a hot iron.

The task of handling cattle also fell to the cowboys who worked on the ranches. A cowboy was a hired hand who looked after cattle. Most were white males, but about one in six was a Mexican male and another one in six was an African-American man. Ranchers supplied each cowboy with a horse. Cowboys also needed saddles, other riding gear, and a *lariat*—a rope made of braided rawhide or twisted grass that was used to capture cattle. On a ranch, cowboys lived in bunkhouses.

When it was time to start a long drive, cowboys rounded up the cattle. A small herd might number 500; the largest herd might contain about 15,000. It usually took 10 men, including a trail boss and a cook, to drive 2,500 cattle. Nearly everything the men needed on the trail was carried in the *chuck wagon*, whose rear opened into the cook's work table. On the trail, cowboys worked up to 18 hours every day of the week. They had to deal with river crossings, angry settlers who did not want the cattle on their land, and prairie fires. They also had to locate enough grass and water for the herd and stop stampedes triggered by thunder or other noises. It would take about four or more months to travel about 1,000 miles.

Most long drives ended in cow towns on railway lines, such as Cheyenne and Dodge City. Some trails continued north to Canada where cattle was also sold. At the end of the drive, cowboys were paid up to $100 for months of hard work. Often, they spent all of their wages in the saloons and stores of the cow towns. In the meantime, the cattle barons made thousands of dollars profit on the sale of the cattle.

More Map Work

Challenge students to do one of the following projects:

- Research the history of the trails shown on the map—the Goodnight-Loving, Western, Chisholm, or Shawnee. Create map pieces to show people, locations, and events.

- Select one of the cow towns on the map. Then, find out when it became a boomtown and its history since then.

Teaching With the Map

1. **What does the map show?** *(It shows four major cattle trails leading north from Texas to the intersection of railway lines or cow towns.)*

2. **Why were cattle herded north?** *(The railroad, on which cattle was loaded and shipped to the East, were up north. Cattle owners could make a huge profit by meeting the growing demand for beef on the East Coast.)*

3. **What was a cowboy?** *(A cowboy was a hired hand who looked after cattle. About two-thirds were white males, one-sixth were African-American men, and one-sixth were Mexican men.)*

4. **What difficulties did cowboys encounter on a cattle drive?** *(Angry settlers, river crossings, wildfires, stampedes, and so on)*

5. **What does the pop-up show?** *(It shows a cow town with a railroad running through it.)*

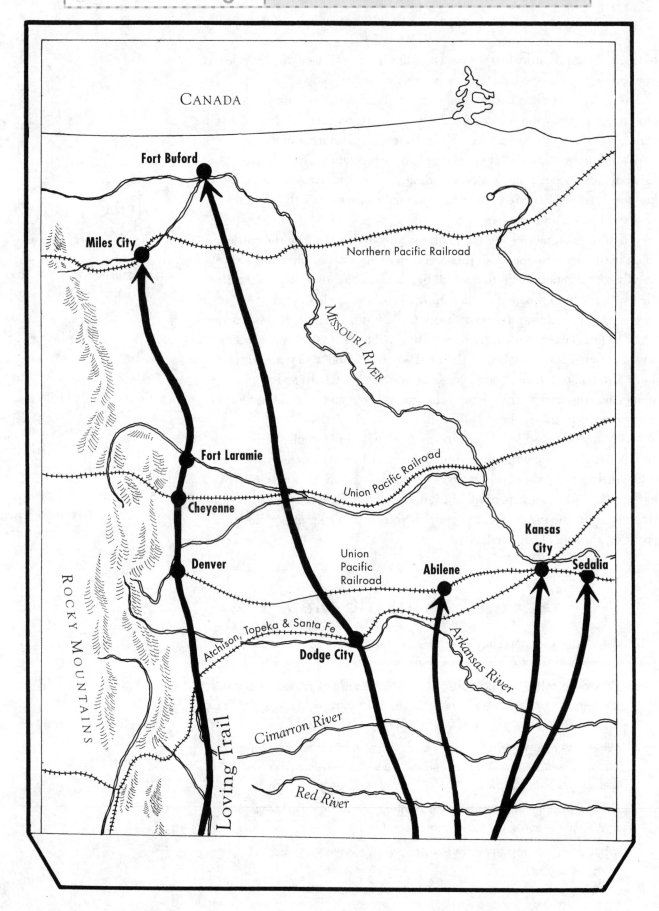

CANADA

Fort Buford

Miles City

Northern Pacific Railroad

MISSOURI RIVER

Fort Laramie

Cheyenne

Union Pacific Railroad

Kansas City

Denver

Union Pacific Railroad

Abilene

Sedalia

ROCKY MOUNTAINS

Atchison, Topeka & Santa Fe

Arkansas River

Dodge City

Loving Trail

Cimarron River

Red River

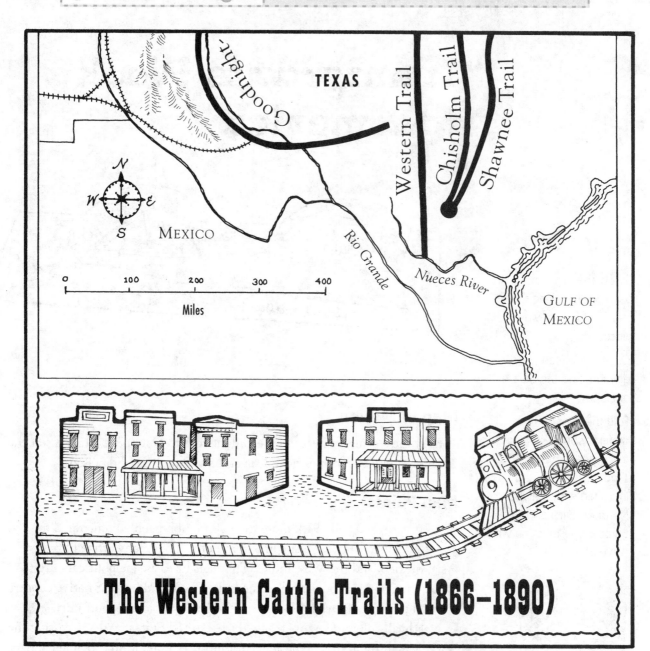

TEXAS

Goodnight-

Western Trail

Chisholm Trail

Shawnee Trail

N
W   E
S

MEXICO

Rio Grande

Nueces River

GULF OF MEXICO

0   100   200   300   400

Miles

The Western Cattle Trails (1866–1890)

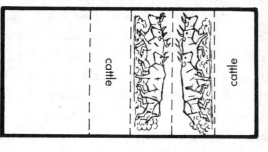

cattle   cattle

Texas longhorn cattle were in demand for their meat.

On the trail, the cook served food at the chuck wagon.

Cowboys were hired to drive cattle north.

Interactive 3-D Maps: American History   Scholastic Teaching Resources

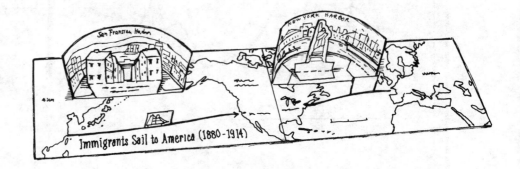

Immigrants Sail to America (1880-1914)

Immigrants Flock to America

Mapmaking

1. Follow the instructions on page 5 for making the map and the moving pieces.

2. Cut out the New York diorama and the Statue of Liberty.

3. Fold the flaps on the diorama forward along the dashed lines. Tape each flap in the indicated spot between North America and Europe. The diorama will curve as shown.

4. Fold the Statue of Liberty so text can be read. Tape in front of the diorama.

5. Repeat steps 2 to 4 for the San Francisco Harbor diorama and the houses piece. Tape these pieces between Asia and North America.

Map in Motion

Insert the steamship near Europe and move it to New York. Then insert the sailing ship (brigantine) near Asia and move it to San Francisco.

Map Points

Between 1880 and 1914, more than 20 million people immigrated to the United States. Most came from Europe, but many arrived from Asia, Mexico, and the West Indies. They sought to escape political unrest, persecution, famine, poverty, and the lack of farmland in their native countries to build new lives in what was seen as the land of golden opportunity.

Nearly all the immigrants reached the United States by sea. Crossing the ocean was a frightening experience for most of them. Many traveled aboard sailing ships called *brigantines* or by steamship. Aboard these vessels, most immigrants (except those who could afford better accommodations) were restricted to the lower decks or *steerage*. Ill passengers who boarded the ships often spread their diseases; others suffered seasickness; still others died before reaching their destinations. It took about three weeks to cross the Pacific Ocean from Asia to San Francisco, and one week to cross the Atlantic Ocean from Europe to New York City. In spite of crowded conditions, homesickness, and fear of the unknown, wave upon wave of immigrants set out with their few possessions, hoping to succeed in a new country that would offer them the chance to develop their talents and skills.

When ships reached New York or San Francisco, a doctor examined each immigrant. Anyone with tuberculosis or other contagious disease was refused admittance to the United States and sent back. Once an immigrant passed the medical examination, a government agent inspected his or her documents and made sure the immigrant was able to work, possessed at least $25, and could answer an interpreter's questions in his or her native language.

Millions of European immigrants passed through Ellis Island, the main center for processing immigrants in New York Harbor. Their spirits were uplifted by the Statue of Liberty, which seemed to welcome them to the land of freedom. Those arriving in San Francisco Harbor after 1910 were processed at Angel Island. Many experienced the harsh reality of detention until government inspectors decided which Asian immigrants to allow into the country. In 1882, Congress passed the Chinese Exclusion Act out of fear that Chinese immigrants willing to work for low pay would take away jobs from Californians. Only Chinese students, tourists, and other non-laborers were allowed to enter the United States.

While some immigrants were greeted by relatives already established in the United States, others had to adapt quickly to a radically different culture and language. They had to find work, a place to live, and people who spoke their native languages and could assist them. Ethnic communities sprang up in cities such as New York, Boston, and San Francisco. They formed a support network for new immigrants and attempted to retain aspects of their native cultures in the new country.

Teaching With the Map

1. **What does the map show?** *(It shows sea routes taken by Asian and European immigrants to the United States.)*

2. **Where did most immigrants arrive?** *(Most European immigrants arrived in New York, and most Asian immigrants arrived in San Francisco.)*

3. **Why did people leave their homes for America?** *(They were seeking better lives and were trying to escape persecution, famine, and other hardships.)*

4. **Describe the voyage to the United States.** *(Most immigrants traveled in the lower decks of brigantines or steamships. Many were ill, others became sick, and some died.)*

5. **What happened when immigrants arrived?** *(Immigrants underwent medical examinations and questioning by government inspectors. Some were sent back because of illness or laws that prevented them from entering the United States.)*

6. **How did immigrants help one another?** *(Relatives met some immigrants when they arrived. Others moved into ethnic communities where people who knew their language and customs helped support them.)*

More Map Work

Challenge students to do one of the following projects:

- Find out when their families first arrived in the United States. Where did their journeys begin? What mode of travel did they use, and about how long did the trip take? Have students show their findings on their maps.

- Research the number of immigrants who came to the United States in any year between 2000 and 2005. What were their countries of origin? What forms of transportation do immigrants today use?

brigantine

brigantine

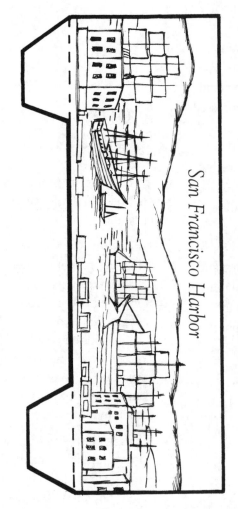

San Francisco Harbor

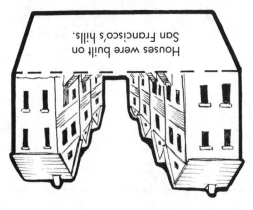

Houses were built on San Francisco's hills.

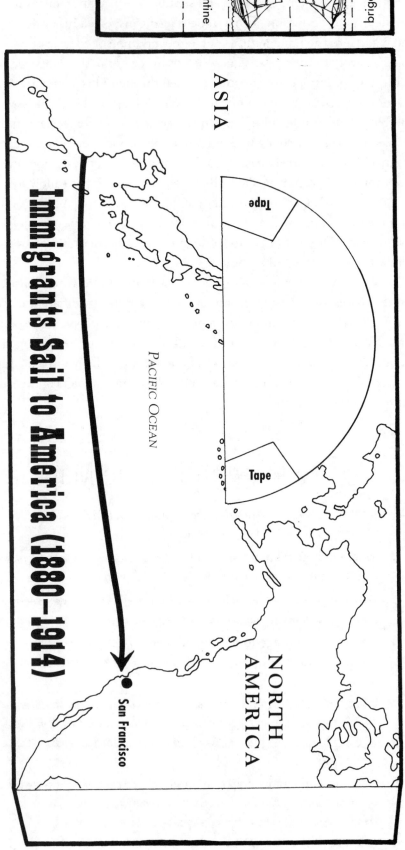

ASIA

Tape

Tape

PACIFIC OCEAN

Immigrants Sail to America (1880–1914)

NORTH AMERICA

San Francisco

Interactive 3-D Maps: American History Scholastic Teaching Resources

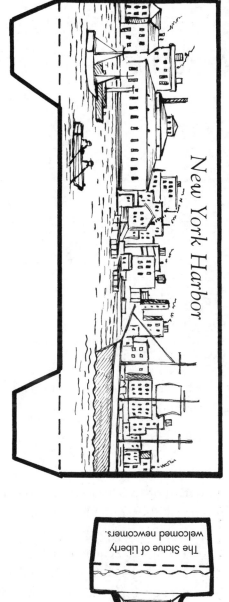

New York Harbor

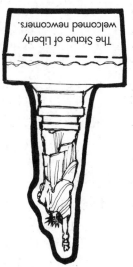

The Statue of Liberty welcomed newcomers.

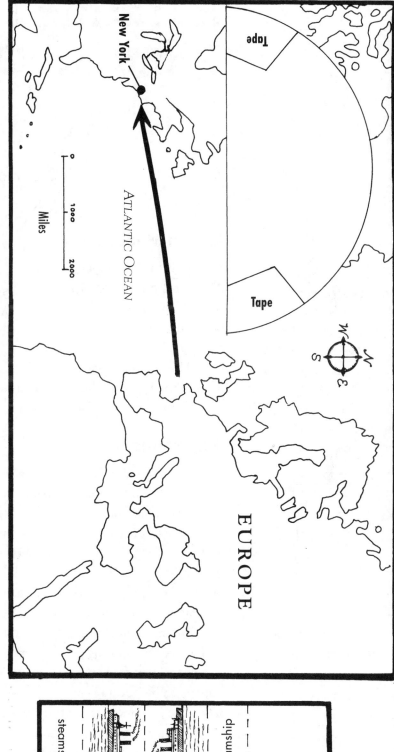

New York

ATLANTIC OCEAN

Miles

0
1000
2000

Tape

Tape

EUROPE

N
W E
S

steamship

steamship

Building the Panama Canal

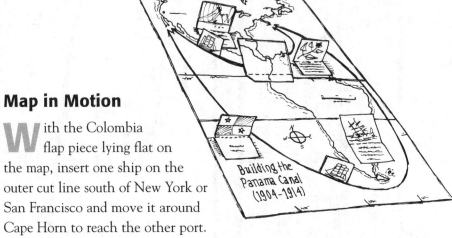

Mapmaking

1. Follow the instructions on page 5 for making the map, the moving pieces, and other pieces. Note: Do not cut open the thin white arrows that extend from New York and San Francisco to the cut lines.

2. Cut out the piece showing Colombia. Tape the lower edge of the flap where indicated on the map.

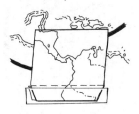

3. Tape the other pieces to the map as follows:

   • the storm piece above Cape Horn

   • the Panama flag above the map title

4. When the flap is lifted up, place the mosquitoes and quinine pieces without obstructing the inner cut line.

Map in Motion

With the Colombia flap piece lying flat on the map, insert one ship on the outer cut line south of New York or San Francisco and move it around Cape Horn to reach the other port. Then raise the Colombia flap and insert the other ship on the inner line and move it through the Panama Canal to its destination.

Map Points

By the end of the 19th century, the United States government was determined to transform the country into a world power. Although the United States modernized the Navy and established naval bases in the West Indies and Hawaii, it still needed a means to shorten ocean travel time between the East and West Coasts of the nation, especially in times of war. A merchant or military ship sailing out of New York Harbor had to travel about 13,000 miles around the tip of South America to reach San Francisco. The length of the trip depended on winds and ocean currents as well as the notorious storms that made sailing around South America so treacherous.

The idea of building a canal across Central America took shape. Naval engineers identified a possible route across Nicaragua and another one across Panama. The Nicaraguan route was longer, but much of it would transverse a lake. The Panama route, while shorter, would mean crossing swamps and mountains. At the time, Panama was part of Colombia. When the United States Senate voted on the Panama route, negotiations began with Colombia over rights to build the canal. Then, in 1903, Panama rebelled and declared its independence. The new government gave the United States a 10-mile-wide zone in which to build a canal and perpetual rights to use it.

Work on the canal started in 1904 and continued for 10 years. Besides having to dig through miles of rock and dirt, workers had to battle malaria and yellow fever. Each disease is transmitted through the bite of a different mosquito. Despite the use of quinine to treat malaria, more than 5,000 workers died from diseases or work-related accidents.

The 51-mile-long Panama Canal opened for business on August 15, 1914. It was built with locks. (See page 59 for how locks work.) Ships entering from the Atlantic Ocean sailed through mountains and across lakes until they reached the Pacific Ocean and vice versa. The canal reduced the distance a ship had to travel between New York and San Francisco by almost 8,000 miles. Ships traveling between New York and Japan saved about 4,000 miles, while those sailing from San Francisco had to cover about 5,500 fewer miles to reach Europe. The canal helped increase trade between Atlantic and Pacific coast cities in the United States and between the United States and its southern neighbors.

A few weeks after the Panama Canal was completed, World War I broke out in Europe. The canal helped the nation feel more secure militarily. In 1999, the United States returned control of the Panama Canal and the Canal Zone to Panama.

Teaching With the Map

1. **What does the map show?** (It shows the sailing routes between New York and San Francisco before and after the building of the Panama Canal.)

2. **Why did the United States want to build a canal across Central America?** (A canal would cut down sea travel time between East and West Coast ports. Ships could avoid making the dangerous trip around South America.)

3. **How did the United States gain the Canal Zone?** (After declaring its independence from Colombia, Panama gave the United States a zone in which to build a canal.)

4. **What difficulties did workers face in building the canal?** (They had to dig through miles of rocks and dirt and battle deadly diseases, such as malaria and yellow fever.)

5. **How did the Panama Canal alter travel?** (Not only did the canal reduce the travel distance between the East and West Coasts of the United States by thousands of miles, it also cut the travel distance between Asia and the East Coast and the West Coast and Europe.)

6. **Who owns the Panama Canal today, and why?** (Panama does. In 1999, the United States returned control of the canal and the Canal Zone to Panama.)

More Map Work

Challenge students to learn more about the Panama Canal by researching subjects such as the following:

- French attempts to build a canal

- Drs. Ross, Gorgas, and Reed and their fight against malaria and yellow fever

- gold and silver workers on the Panama Canal and a typical work day

- President Theodore Roosevelt's visit to Panama

- physical and human-made features of Panama and the Panama Canal, including the Pedro Miguel and Miraflores Locks, Gatun Lake, Miraflores Lake, the Gaillard Cut, and the mountains

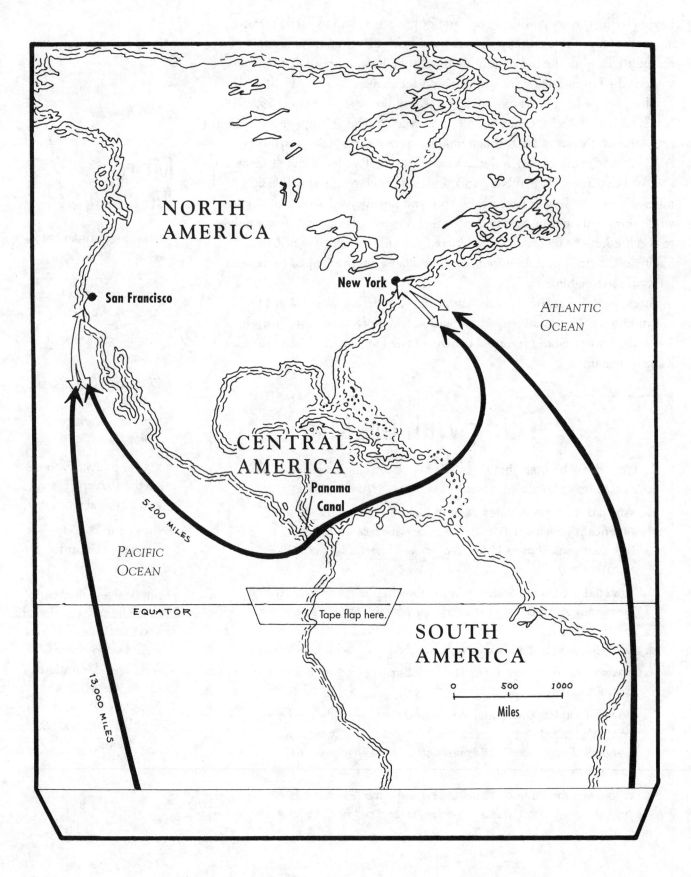

NORTH
AMERICA

San Francisco

New York

ATLANTIC
OCEAN

5200 MILES

CENTRAL
AMERICA

Panama
Canal

PACIFIC
OCEAN

EQUATOR

Tape flap here.

SOUTH
AMERICA

13,000 MILES

0   500   1000
Miles

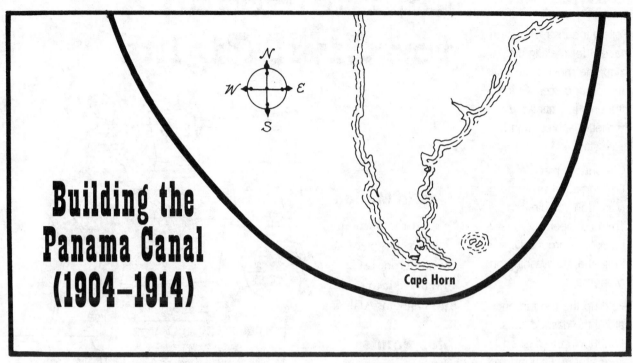

Building the Panama Canal (1904–1914)

Cape Horn

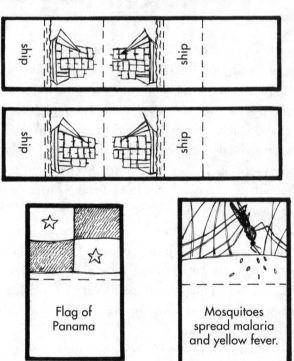

ship ship

ship ship

Many ships rounding Cape Horn sank in storms.

Quinine, from the chinchona tree, is used to treat malaria.

Flag of Panama

Mosquitoes spread malaria and yellow fever.

COLOMBIA

Mapmaking

1. Follow the instructions on page 5 for making the map, the moving pieces, and other pieces. Guide students in writing the two-letter abbreviation for each state.

2. Cut out the piece of Dr. King addressing the March on Washington. Then cut open the heavy black lines around Dr. King and the Washington Monument.

3. Fold up the monument along the dashed lines. Fold down the dashed lines around Dr. King and above the monument. Fold under TAPE A and TAPE B along the dashed lines, as shown.

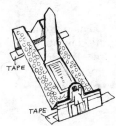

4. Tape the piece on the map where indicated.

5. Tape the other pieces to the map as follows:

   • Malcolm X in the upper right-hand corner

   • Dr. King over TN

   • Rosa Parks over AL

   • dog and fire hose pieces over MS and GA

   • We Shall Overcome button above map title

On the Road for Civil Rights

ON THE ROAD FOR CIVIL RIGHTS (1961–1965)

The March on Washington

Map in Motion

Insert the freedom riders' bus piece at Washington, D.C., and move it toward Birmingham, Alabama.

Map Points

While slavery was abolished during the Civil War, hatred and prejudice were not. Instead of ensuring that African Americans were treated as equals, federal, state, and local governments from Reconstruction to the 1950s devised ways of denying them the freedoms guaranteed by the Constitution. Racial stereotypes abounded as did Jim Crow laws aimed at keeping whites and blacks separated. The Supreme Court decision in the 1896 *Plessy v. Ferguson* case allowed the segregation of the colored races as long as they were accorded separate but equal facilities. Even in northern cities where whites prided themselves on having abolished slavery, African Americans could find places to live only in all-black neighborhoods.

After World War II, the plight of African Americans denied equal rights and opportunities became more difficult to ignore. In 1954, the Supreme Court declared segregation unconstitutional in the case of African-American children who were denied admission to all-white schools in Topeka, Kansas. A year later, Rosa Parks was arrested in Montgomery, Alabama, for refusing to give up her seat on a bus to a white man.

While most states complied with the 1954 Supreme Court decision, some resisted. In 1957, President Dwight D. Eisenhower had to send in federal troops in Arkansas to integrate an all-white high school. Despite a series of showdowns, nonviolent protests led by Dr. Martin Luther King, Jr., and other activists, and staged sit-ins at segregated lunch counters and bus terminals, Congress failed to pass civil-rights legislation, including laws that guarantee the rights of African Americans to vote.

In the early 1960s, buses carrying *freedom riders* took to the road. They transported activists to segregated cities and towns such as Birmingham, Alabama. The activists' aim was to focus media coverage on the civil-rights issue and force President John F. Kennedy to protect their right to protest against the way African Americans were treated. Some buses were bombed. On others, riders were pulled off and beaten by mobs of angry whites. Still other protesters were knocked down by water from fire hoses or attacked by police dogs. Newspapers nationwide expressed outrage, and the president sent hundreds of U.S. Marshals to protect the freedom riders.

President Kennedy and his administration began to take a more active role in civil rights. In 1963, he pressured Congress to pass a comprehensive civil-rights bill. More than 250,000 people marched on Washington, D.C., gathering between the Lincoln and Washington Monuments to hear speaker after speaker demand the bill's passage. Dr. King delivered his "I Have a Dream" speech, a defining moment in American history.

In July 1964, President Lyndon B. Johnson signed the Civil Rights Act of 1964, prohibiting discrimination based on race, religion, gender, or national origin. The fight for civil rights was far from over. In 1965, civil-rights activist Malcolm X was assassinated in New York City. Three years later, Dr. King was slain in Memphis, Tennessee.

More Map Work

Challenge students to research efforts to register African Americans to vote in Mississippi in 1964 and in Selma, Alabama, in 1964 and 1965. Have them map the 1965 march from Selma to Montgomery, Alabama's state capital. Also, ask students to create a time line showing important events in the civil-rights movement.

Teaching With the Map

1. **What does the map show?** *(It shows the route taken by freedom riders on a bus from Washington, D.C., to Birmingham, Alabama.)*

2. **How were African Americans treated during the first half of the 20th century?** *(They were denied equal rights and opportunities. In most cities and towns, they were made to live segregated from whites.)*

3. **What historical decision did the Supreme Court make in 1954?** *(It declared that segregation is unconstitutional.)*

4. **Why did freedom riders take to the road in the 1960s?** *(They wanted to turn national attention to the issue of civil rights and force President Kennedy to protect their rights to protest.)*

5. **What happened to freedom riders in places such as Birmingham, Alabama?** *(Some were beaten, attacked by dogs, and knocked down by water jets.)*

6. **What was the March on Washington?** *(In 1963, more than 250,000 people marched on Washington, D.C., in support of civil-rights legislation.)*

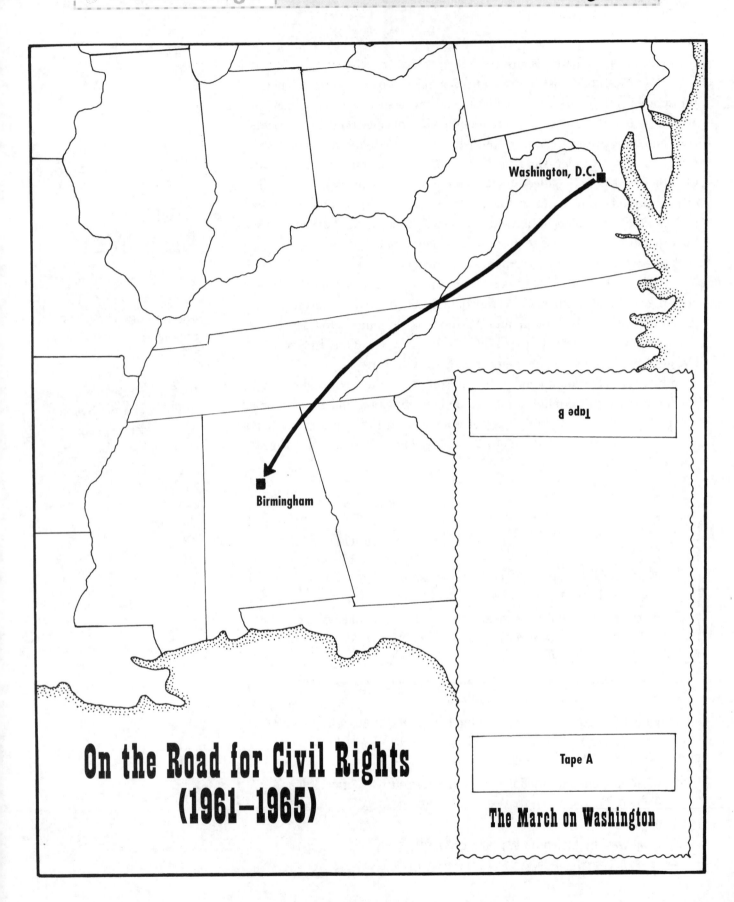

Washington, D.C.

Tape B

Birmingham

On the Road for Civil Rights
(1961–1965)

Tape A

The March on Washington

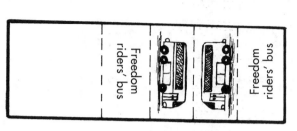

Freedom riders' bus

Freedom riders' bus

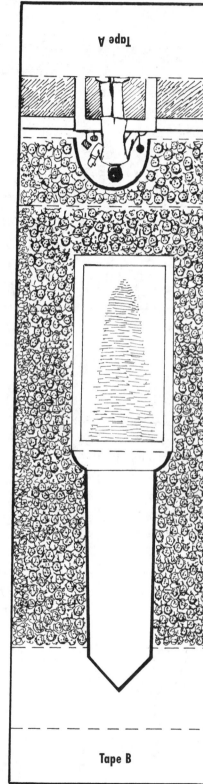

Tape A

Tape B

WE SHALL OVERCOME

Some civil rights activists were attacked by police dogs.

In 1955, Rosa Parks refused to give up her bus seat.

Malcolm X was a leader in the fight against racism.

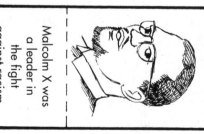

Dr. King preached peaceful resistance as a way to end racial injustice.

Water jets from fire hoses were turned on protesters.

Mapmaking

1. Follow the instructions on page 5 for making the map.

2. Cut out the *Apollo 11* piece. Fold along the dashed lines as shown.

3. Insert the *Apollo 11* piece into the cut-open arrow.

4. Cut out the lunar module piece. Fold it in half along the dashed midline. Next, fold the end sections down and tape them together to form a triangular piece, as shown.

5. Tape the footprint piece near the lunar module on the moon.

From Earth to the Moon

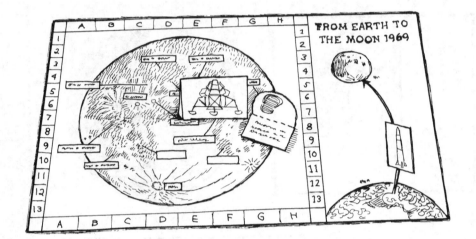

Map in Motion

Insert the *Apollo 11* piece on Earth and move it to the moon. Then lower the lunar module piece to coordinate F7 on the moon.

Map Points

The moon is Earth's closest neighbor in space. About one-quarter the size of our planet, the moon is about 239,000 miles away and orbits Earth once every 28 days. Unlike the sun, the moon does not make its own light. Instead, the moon reflects sunlight. There is no life on the moon because it has no atmosphere—meaning it has no air or weather—or water. It does have rugged mountain ranges called *lunar highlands* and smooth dark plains. The astronomer Galileo named these plains *maria* (MAR-ee-uh), which means "seas" in Latin, because from Earth they looked as if they were filled with water. However, scientists now know that the darkness comes from hardened lava that spewed out of lunar volcanoes billions of years ago. Countless craters—formed by meteorites, asteroids, and comets crashing into it—also cover the moon's surface.

The race to the moon started October 4, 1957, when the former Soviet Union launched the first artificial unmanned satellite, *Sputnik*, into orbit around Earth. It was launched with a missile powerful enough to attack the United States in the event of a nuclear war. Americans, fearing such a nuclear attack, demanded that the United States not fall behind the Soviets in science and technology. The space race was on.

In January 1958, the United States successfully launched an unmanned satellite. In 1959, a Soviet probe impacted the moon's surface; then in 1961, the Soviets scored another first when Yuri Gagarin became the first human to circle Earth in a spacecraft. One month later, American astronaut Alan Shepard traveled into space for 15 minutes. Although Shepard's flight was brief, it demonstrated to Americans that President Kennedy's call for landing an American on the moon before 1970 could be achieved.

In February 1962, John Glenn became the first American to orbit Earth; in June 1963, Soviet astronaut Valentina Tereshkova became the first woman in space. The race to land a person on the moon ended on July 20, 1969, when American astronaut Neil Armstrong stepped down from the lunar module *Eagle* onto the surface of the moon. Armstrong, Edwin Aldrin, and Michael Collins had taken off from Cape Canaveral, Florida, on July 19 in *Apollo 11*, a three-stage rocket. While Collins remained in the command module orbiting the moon, Armstrong and Aldrin spent two-and-a-half hours on the moon collecting rock samples, taking pictures, setting up experiments, planting the American flag, and talking to President Richard Nixon via telephone. After lifting off from the moon in the *Eagle*, they joined Collins in the command module and returned to Earth on July 24, 1969.

Teaching With the Map

1. **What does the map show?** (It shows Apollo 11 *moving from Earth to the moon and the lunar module setting down on the moon's surface.*)

2. **Based on the coordinates on the map of the moon, where did the lunar module set down?** (It set down in the Sea of Tranquility.)

3. **What are the "seas" on the moon made of?** (They are made of hardened lava that spewed out of volcanoes billions of years ago.)

4. **How is the moon different from Earth?** (The moon has no life; it has no water, air, weather, or atmosphere; it's covered with craters made by meteorites.)

5. **What was the space race?** (It was a competition between the former Soviet Union and the United States to be the most advanced country in science and technology and to be the first to orbit and land on the moon.)

6. **Who were the first people to walk on the moon, and what did they do?** (American Neil Armstrong was the first person to walk on the moon. Edwin Aldrin was the second. Both astronauts collected rock samples, took pictures, set up experiments, planted an American flag, and spoke to President Nixon before lifting off from the lunar surface.)

More Map Work

Divide the class into groups, and assign a Soviet or American space program such as *Sputnik, Explorer, Mercury, Lunik, Pioneer, Surveyor,* or *Apollo* to each group. Challenge each group to research its program and draw a space map showing each flight that left Earth, where it went, and what it accomplished. You may want to include post-1969 programs including *Soyuz, Salyut, Skylab, Voyager, Mir,* and *Galileo.*

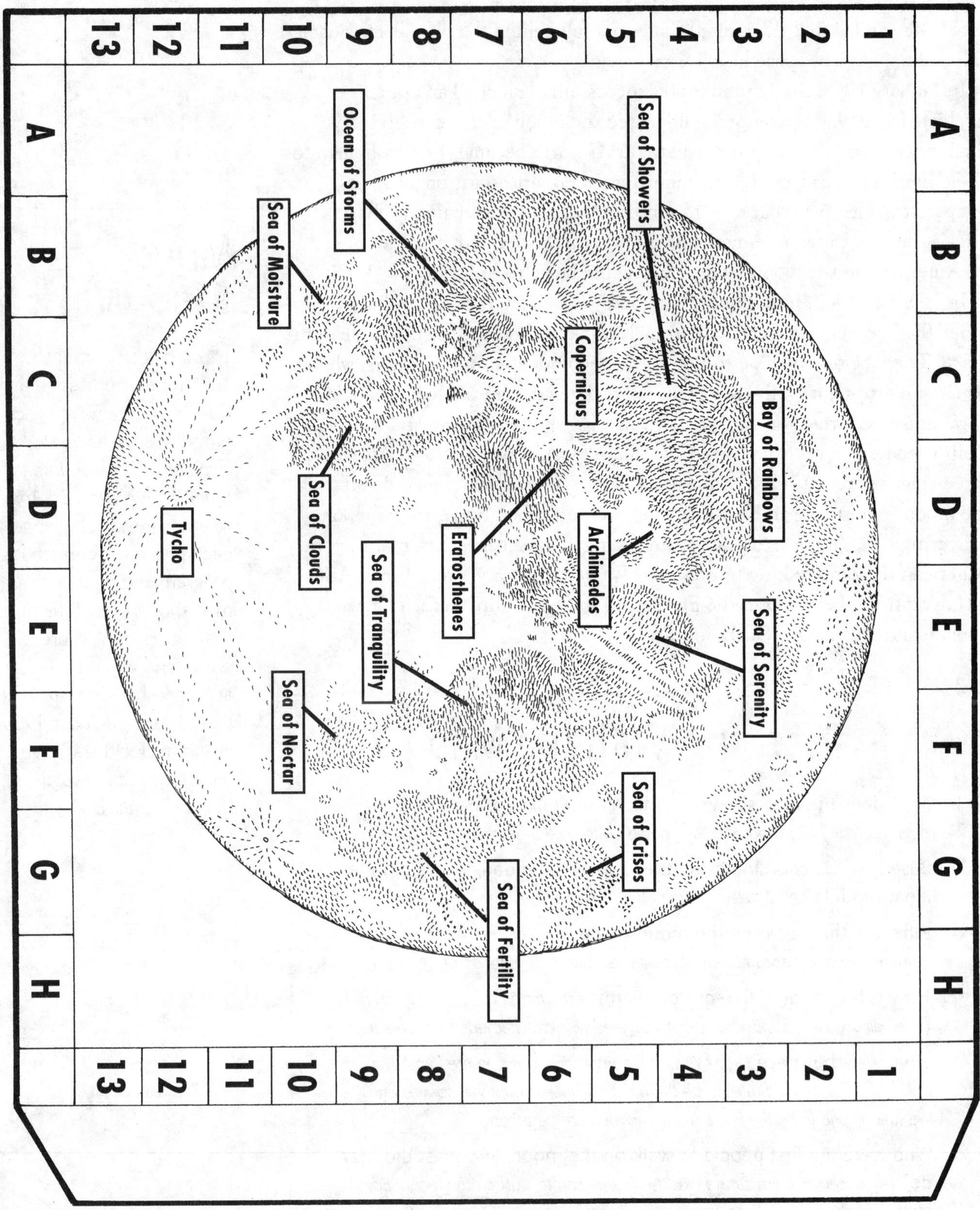

| | 13 | 12 | 11 | 10 | 9 | 8 | 7 | 6 | 5 | 4 | 3 | 2 | 1 | |

Ocean of Storms
Sea of Moisture
Sea of Showers
Copernicus
Bay of Rainbows
Sea of Clouds
Tycho
Eratosthenes
Archimedes
Sea of Tranquility
Sea of Serenity
Sea of Nectar
Sea of Crises
Sea of Fertility

A B C D E F G H

Interactive 3-D Maps: American History   Scholastic Teaching Resources

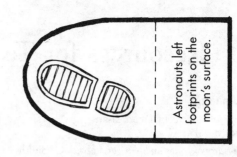

Astronauts left footprints on the moon's surface.

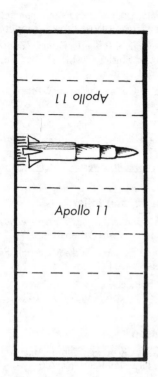

Apollo 11

Apollo 11

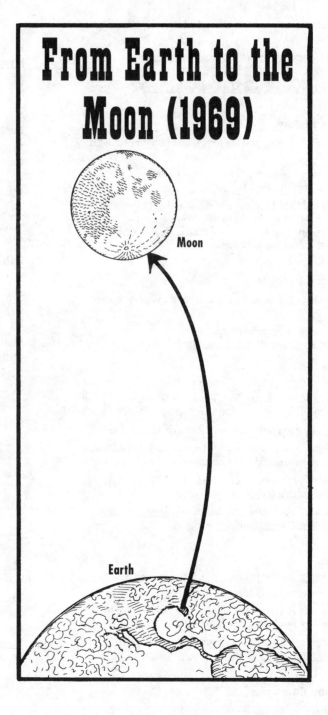

From Earth to the Moon (1969)

Moon

Earth

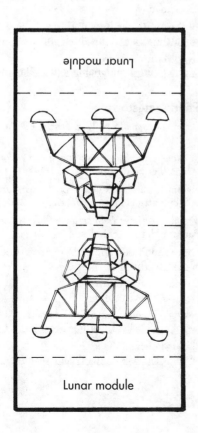

Lunar module

Lunar module

Resources for Teachers and Students

Maps and Mapmaking

How to Draw Maps and Charts by Pam Beasant and Alastair Smith (Scholastic, 1993)

Where Am I? The Story of Maps and Navigation by A.G. Smith (Stoddart Kids, 1997)

Small Worlds: Maps and Mapmaking by Karen Romano Young (Scholastic, 2002)

Library of Congress: http://memory.loc.gov/ammem

Yale University: http://www.library.yale.edu/MapColl/index.html

American History

History of US (11 volumes) by Joy Hakim (Oxford University Press, 1999)

Visiting Our Past: America's Historylands (The National Geographic Society, 1977)

The Settling of North America: The Atlas of Great Migrations into North America from the Ice Age to the Present edited by Helen Hornbeck Tanner, Janice Reiff, John H. Long, Henry F. Dobyn (Macmillan Publishing Co., 1995)

Ice Age and Beringia

The Last Giant of Beringia by Dick O'Neill (Westview Press, 2004)

NOVA America's Stone Age Explorers: http://www.pbs.org/wgbh/nova/stoneage/

Vikings

Vikings: The North Atlantic Saga edited by William H. Fitzhugh and Elisabeth I. Ward (Smithsonian Books, 2000) (for teachers)

The Vikings by Elizabeth Janeway (Random House, 1981)

Vinland Sagas: Norse Discovery of America edited by Magnus Magnusson (Penguin, 1965) (for teachers)

Smithsonian Institution Vikings exhibit: http://www.mnh.si.edu/vikings/start.html

Parks Canada L'Anse aux Meadows: http://www.pc.gc.ca/lhn-nhs/nl/meadows/natcul/hist_e.asp

Columbus

The Four Voyages of Christopher Columbus compiled by J.M. Cohen (Penguin, 1992) (for teachers)

Pedro's Journal: A Voyage with Christopher Columbus August 3, 1492–February 14, 1493 (Boyds Mills Press, 1991)

Fordham University (excerpts from Columbus's journal): http://www.fordham.edu/halsall/source/columbus1.html

Cortés and Coronado

The Discovery and Conquest of Mexico: 1517–1521 by Bernal Diaz del Castillo (Da Capo Press, 2003)

Cortés and the Conquest of Mexico by the Spaniards in 1521 by B.G. Herzog and Margaret Wise Brown (Linnet Books, 1988)

The Coronado Expedition: From the Distance of 460 Years edited by Richard Flint and Shirley Cushing Flint (University of New Mexico Press, 2003)

Francisco Vasquez de Coronado by Jim Whiting (Mitchell Lane Publishers, 2002)

PBS *Conquistadors*: http://www.pbs.org/conquistadors/cortes/cortes_flat.html

PBS *The West*: http://www.pbs.org/weta/thewest/people/a_c/coronado.htm

Cartier, Marquette, and Joliet

Braving the North Atlantic: Jacques Cartier's Voyage to America by Delno West and Jean West (Atheneum, 1996)

Joliet and Marquette: Explorers of the Mississippi River by Daniel E. Harmon (Chelsea House Publications, 2001)

Museum of New France: http://www.civilization.ca/vmnf/explor/explcd_e.html

Cabot and Hudson

John Cabot and the Rediscovery of North America by Charles J. Shields (Chelsea Hose Publications, 2001)

Beyond the Sea of Ice: The Voyages of Henry Hudson by Joan Elizabeth Goodman (Mikaya Press, 1999)

Matthew of Bristol (Great Britain Trust): http://www.matthew.co.uk/home/home.html

Hudson River Maritime Museum: http://www.ulster.net/~hrmm/halfmoon/1609moon.htm

Roanoke and Jamestown

The Lost Colony of Roanoke by Jean Fritz (G.P. Putnam's Sons, 2004)

Our Strange New Land: Elizabeth's Jamestown Colony Diary, Book One by Patricia Herme (Scholastic, 2001)

The Starving Time: Elizabeth's Diary, Book Two, Jamestown, Virginia 1609 by Patricia Herme (Scholastic, 2002)

Season of Promise: Elizabeth's Jamestown Colony Diary, Book Three by Patricia Herme (Scholastic, 2002)

Association for the Preservation of Virginia Antiquities: http://www.apva.org/history/

The Virtual Jamestown Archive: http://www.virtualjamestown.org/

PBS Alan Alda's *Scientific American Frontiers*: http://www.pbs.org/saf/1203/features/pocahontas.htm

Virginia Places (Powhatan's Confederacy) http://www.virginiaplaces.org/nativeamerican/anglopowhatan.html

Pilgrims

Homes in the Wilderness: A Pilgrim's Journal of the Plymouth Plantation in 1620 by William Bradford, edited by Margaret Wise Brown (Linnet Books, 1988)

1621: A New Look at Thanksgiving by Margaret M. Bruchac and Catherine O'Neill Grace (National Geographic Society, 2001)

Plimoth Plantation: http://www.plimoth.org/

The Avalon Project at the Yale Law Center (Mayflower Compact): http://www.yale.edu/lawweb/avalon/amerdoc/mayflower.htm

Slave Trade

Middle Passage by Charles Johnson (Simon & Schuster, 1990) (for teachers)

Freedom's Sons: The True Story of the Amistad Mutiny by Suzanne Jurmain (HarperCollins, 1998)

Slave Ship: The Story of the Henrietta Marie by George Sullivan (Dutton Books, 1994)

The Wreck of the *Henrietta Marie*: http://www.melfisher.org/henriettamarie/overview.htm

Amistad at Mystic Seaport: http://www.amistad.org/

Pirates

The Pirate's Handbook by Margarette Lincoln (Cobblehill Books, 1995)

The Pirates Own Book: Authentic Narratives of the Most Celebrated Sea Robbers edited by Marine Research Society (Dover, 1993) (for teachers)

National Geographic Society for Kids: http://www.nationalgeographic.com/pirates/

Paul Revere

Paul Revere's Ride by David Hackett Fischer (Oxford University Press, 1995) (young adult-adult)

America's Paul Revere by Esther Hopkins Forbes (Houghton Mifflin, 1990)

The Paul Revere House: http://www.paulreverehouse.org/

National Park Service Minute Man National Historic Park: http://www.nps.gov/mima/index.htm

George Washington

Washington's Crossing by David Hackett Fischer (Oxford University Press, 2004) (young adult-adult)

George Washington's Socks by Elvira Woodruff (Scholastic, 1993)

Washington Crossing State Park: http://www.cr.nps.gov/nr/travel/delaware/was.htm

NPR Washington Crossing the Delaware: http://www.npr.org/programs/morning/features/patc/georgewashington

Lewis & Clark

Lewis and Clark's West: William Clark's 1810 Master Map of the American West by William Clark (University Press of New England, 2004)

Lewis and Clark: The Journey of the Corps of Discovery by Dayton Duncan and Ken Burns (Alfred A. Knopf, 1999)

National Geographic Society Guide to the Lewis and Clark Trail by Thomas Schmidt (National Geographic Society, 2002)

PBS Lewis and Clark: The Corps of Discovery: http://www.pbs.org/lewisandclark/

National Geographic Society: http://www.nationalgeographic.com/lewisandclark/

National Park Service: http://www.nps.gov/lecl/

Erie Canal

The Erie Canal Reader, 1790–1950 edited by Roger Hecht (Syracuse University Pres, 2003) (for teachers)

Erie Canal: Canoeing America's Great Waterway by Peter Lourie (Boyds Mills Press, 1997)

Erie Canal Home Page: http://www.eriecanal.org/

Trail of Tears

The Journal of Jesse Smoke: A Cherokee Boy, the Trail of Tears, 1838 by Joseph Bruchac (Scholastic, 2001)

Voices from the Trail of Tears edited by Vicki Rozema (John F. Blair, 2003) (for teachers)

The Cherokee Nation: http://www.cherokee.org/Culture/HistoryCat.asp?Cat=TOT

Trail of Tears National Historic Site: http://www.nps.gov/trte/TRTE/home.htm

Oregon Trail

The Oregon Trail by Francis Parkman (National Geographic Society, 2002)

Fantastic Facts about the Oregon Trail by Michael T. Trinklein (Trinklein Publishing, 1995)

End of the Oregon Trail Interpretive Center: http://www.endoftheoregontrail.org/wagons.html

National Park Service Mormon Trail: http://www.nps.gov/mopi/mopi/mopi_home.htm

Mississippi River

Steamboats on the Mississippi by Ralph K. Andrist (Troll Communications, 1988)

Life on the Mississippi by Mark Twain (Oxford University Press, 1996)

Mark Twain at Large: The Mississippi River (University of California at Berkeley Library): http://bancroft.berkeley.edu/Exhibits/MTP/mississippi.html

Underground Railroad

North Star to Freedom by Gena K. Correll (Delacorte Press, 1997)

Freedom Roads: Searching for the Underground Railroad by Joyce Hansen and Gary McGowan (Cricket Books, 2003)

National Geographic Online:
http://www.nationalgeographic.com/railroad/

National Park Service National Underground Railroad Network to Freedom:
http://209.10.16.21/TEMPLATE/FrontEnd/index.cfm

Civil War Blockade

Duel of the Ironclads by Patrick O'Brien (Walker & Co., 2003)

Raising the Hunley by Brian Hicks and Schuyler Kropf (Presidio Press, 2003) (young adult-adult)

USN Ships:

U.S.S. *Monitor*: http://www.history.navy.mil/photos/sh-usn/usnsh-m/monitor.htm

C.S.S. *Virginia*: http://www.history.navy.mil/photos/sh-us-cs/csa-sh/csash-sz/virginia.htm

H.L. Hunley: http://www.history.navy.mil/branches/org12-3.htm

Telegraph & Pony Express

The Travel Guide to the Pony Express Trail by Joe Bensen (Falcon, 1995)

Riders of the Pony Express by Ralph Moody (University of Nebraska Press, 2004) (young adult)

Locust Grove: The Samuel Morse Historic Site:
http://www.morsehistoricsite.org/

Pony Express History: http://www.ponyexpress.org/history.htm

Transcontinental Railroad

Full Steam Ahead: The Race to Build a Transcontinental Railroad by Rhoda Blumberg (Scholastic, 1996)

Hear That Lonesome Whistle Blow by Dee Brown (Owl Books, 2001) (for teachers)

The Central Pacific Railroad Photographic History Museum:
http://www.cprr.org/

Union Pacific Railroad History and Photos:
http://www.uprr.com/aboutup/history/index.shtml

Cattle Trails

Cowboys and Cattle Drives by Eric Oatman (National Geographic Society, 2004)

Cowboys and Longhorns: A Portrait of a Long Drive by Jerry Stanley (Crown Books for Young Readers, 2003)

Texas State Historical Association Online Handbook Cattle Trailing:
http://www.tsha.utexas.edu/handbook/online/articles/CC/ayc1.html

Western Trail:
http://www.tsha.utexas.edu/handbook/online/articles/WW/ayw2.html

Goodnight-Loving Trail:
http://www.tsha.utexas.edu/handbook/online/articles/GG/ayg2.html

Chisholm Trail:
http://www.tsha.utexas.edu/handbook/online/articles/CC/ayc2.html

Shawnee Trail:
http://www.tsha.utexas.edu/handbook/online/articles/SS/ays2.html

Ellis Island & Angel Island

Kai's Journey to the Gold Mountain: An Angel Island Story by Katrina Saltonstall Currier (Angel Island Association, 2004)

An Ellis Island Collection: Artifacts from the Immigrant Experience by Brad Tuttle (Chronicle Books, 2004)

The Statue of Liberty-Ellis Island Foundation:
http://www.ellisisland.org/

Angel Island Immigration Station Foundation:
http://www.aiisf.org/history

Panama Canal

The Panama Canal by Elizabeth Mann (Mikaya Press, 1998)

Path Between the Seas: The Creation of the Panama Canal, 1870–1914 by David McCullough (Simon & Schuster, 2004) (for teachers)

Smithsonian Institution: Make the Dirt Fly:
http://www.sil.si.edu/Exhibitions/Make-the-Dirt-Fly/index.html

Civil Rights

Time of Change: Civil Rights Photographs, 1961–1965 by Bruce Davidson (St. Ann's Press, 2002)

Oh, Freedom!: Kids Talk About the Civil Rights Movement With the People Who Made It Happen by Casey King and Linda Barrett Osborne (Rebound by Sagebrush, 1999)

American Radio Works (Little Rock):
http://americanradioworks.publicradio.org/features/marshall/littlerock1.html

We Shall Overcome: Historic Places in the Civil Rights Movement National Register Travel Itinerary:
http://www.cr.nps.gov/nr/travel/civilrights/index.htm

Space Flight

Escape from Earth: Voyages Through Time by Peter Ackroyd (DK Publishing Inc., 2004)

The Man Who Went to the Far Side of the Moon: The Story of Apollo 11 Astronaut Michael Collins by Bea Uusma Schyffert (Chronicle Books, 2003)

Stardate: University of Texas McDonald Observatory:
http://stardate.org/resources/ssguide/moon.html

NASA: http://www.nasa.gov